Culinary Arts Institute

THE
OUTDOOR
COOKBOOK

THE
OUTDOOR

THE OUTDOOR COOKBOOK

**Barbara MacDonald
and the Culinary Arts Institute Staff:**

Helen Geist: Director • Sherrill Corley: Editor
Edward Finnegan: Executive Editor • Charles Bozett: Art Director
Ethel La Roche: Editorial Assistant • Ivanka Simatic: Recipe Tester
Laurel DiGangi: Art Coordinator • Fritz Adler: Layout
Malinda Miller: Copy Editor

Book designed by Charles Bozett

Illustrations by Dev Appleyard

COOKBOOK

Culinary Arts Institute

1727 South Indiana Avenue, Chicago, Illinois 60616

Library of Congress Catalog Card Number: 75-10711
International Standard Book Number: 0-8326-0545-X

PHOTO ACKNOWLEDGMENTS

Adolph's Ltd.; Alaska King Crab; American Dairy Association;
Charcoal Briquet Institute; Florida Department of Citrus;
Halibut Association of North America; The McIlhenny Company (Tabasco);
Reynolds Metals Company; Washington State Fruit Commission.

FOREWORD

Most of us are blessed with all the comforts of home—with everything including the kitchen sink at our disposal (and sometimes even a disposal!). So why do we choose to leave it all behind and cook out of doors? There has to be a good reason. If the happy conversation and relaxed atmosphere around the grill are any clue, it must be that cooking outdoors is more fun.

That's the premise of this book. Outdoor cooking and eating can be fun, and will be, if the chef is armed with know-how to keep the job simple. The helps and recipes offered here are just the background the cook will need.

There are several different styles of outdoor cooking, and the expertise in one doesn't necessarily overlap into the other areas. You may rate honors at the backyard grill, for example, and find campsite or beach-side cooking a whole new kettle of fish.

So, gathered here are the finer points of fresh-air cooking, examined in detail for the backyard barbecue chef, the picnicker away from home, the camper and sailor who travel even further afield, and finally, for the backpacker who wants to rough it back to real nature. Each has its own set of routines and techniques; each has its own special reward—the fun that makes it all worthwhile.

THE DAILY FOUR—AND MORE

When outdoor cooking becomes more than a one-meal proposition, such as when you're on vacation, consult this Daily Food Guide and do some advance planning. The members of your family will probably be extra-active on the trip, so meals must furnish plenty of energy and nutrients.

Even if you rarely make advance meal plans at home, it's a good idea to have them on the road. After all, you won't have the freezer or pantry door to open for some forgotten "must." You'll have to remember everything in advance, so you can shop and pack for the trip.

Having plans makes cooking away from home go faster, too. No wonder the Scouts, those famous campers, say "Be Prepared!"

The following guide shows the number of servings needed in daily meals from the four basic food groups. Growing children and active people are among those lucky individuals who have higher nutrient needs and can supplement meals with seconds and snacks. The category below called "Other" includes those fun foods not covered by the basic four, but which are important to mealtime enjoyment. Such items as candy, soft drinks, alcoholic beverages, ice cream, butter, and salad dressings come under the "Other" heading.

DAILY FOOD GUIDE

By Food Groups	child	pre-teen & teen	adult	aging adult
MILK GROUP cups of milk or equivalents in milk products (cheese and ice cream)	3–4	4 or more	2	2
MEAT GROUP 3 oz. serving meat, fish, shellfish or poultry; 2 eggs; 1 cup cooked dried beans, peas or lentils; ¼ cup peanut butter	1–2	3 or more	2	2
FRUIT AND VEGETABLE GROUP servings of C-rich fruits and vegetables	1	1–2	1	1–2
servings of A-rich fruits and vegetables	1	2	1	1
servings of potatoes, other fruits and vegetables	2	1	2	0–1
BREAD AND CEREAL GROUP servings of whole grain or enriched bread or cereal, baked goods, macaroni	3–4	4 or more	3–4	2–3
OTHER tablespoons of fat (oil, butter, margarine)	2	2–4	2–3	1–2

Water or liquid equivalent to make 3 to 5 cups total daily intake.

(Chart adapted from American Medical Association and reprinted with permission.)

CONTENTS

BARBECUING KNOW-HOW

The basics of barbecuing are really quite easy. You'll need cooking and serving equipment, fuel and food, and a place to eat. But within that framework, the choices are anything but easy!

The barbecue gear you'll find in the stores ranges from the simple to the sumptuous, so it pays to compare and to limit purchases to those that are essential. If, after experimenting, you find that your enjoyment of barbecuing merits additional investment, then move up to the fancier equipment. The cost of the grill alone can range from a few dollars to several hundred.

Some outdoor chefs have cooked for years on the same bargain-department grill, never feeling the urge to splurge. But others who have decided to go first class have found that costlier units do offer worthwhile refinements.

And the money invested initially in that small grill is not lost, even if you graduate to the grand grill. It can be used as a second cooking surface for appetizers, or for hot dogs for the children while some gourmet specialty cooks for the adults.

Here is some background on basic barbecue equipment and the sort of choices you can expect to find on the market.

COOKING EQUIPMENT

The grill you choose will depend on the fuel you use. Grills come in models using charcoal briquets, gas, or electricity. Assuming that you will want to work your way up, here is a look at charcoal grills, beginning with the simplest.

THE BRAZIER

The most basic brazier is a fire bowl set on three or four legs, with a grid on top to hold the food. Only slightly fancier is the brazier on two wheels to make the grill mobile. A most helpful feature is a lever for adjusting grid height. This allows the chef to move the food closer to, or farther from, the glowing coals.

Other features sometimes found on braziers are the wind screen, half hood, and rotisserie. Some braziers come with a draft control at the bottom of the fire bowl to help control heat.

Once you understand the basics of the barbecue grill, it's simple enough to make your own. Firebox and grid are the essentials.

For the firebox, any heavy, fireproof material will do. Look around and see what you can put into service. An oversize cast-iron skillet will work. Place it on a base of bricks and line with aluminum foil before adding the briquets.

A clay flower pot and saucer will pinch-hit for a brazier, too. Line the pot with foil up to the brim and fill a little over half full with sand or gravel. Add another layer of foil. This will hold a half dozen or so briquets to make a nifty cooker for an individual meat serving or several appetizers.

A sandy beach makes a natural firebox; just outline the cooking area with bricks or rocks before starting the fire.

The grid to top your improvised firebox can be wire mesh cut to size, or a cake rack. Or—use your ingenuity, a priceless commodity for the outdoor cook. That's particularly true when

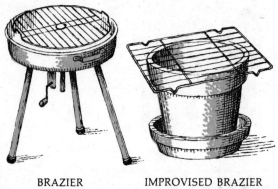

BRAZIER   IMPROVISED BRAZIER
WITH CAKE RACK

you're cooking away from home and all the comforts of the backyard patio.

THE HIBACHI

"Hibachi" means "fire basin" in Japanese. This portable charcoal burner is usually made of cast iron, but can also be found in aluminum. It comes in many sizes; the smaller ones can be used indoors if placed close to an open window or set in a fireplace with an open draft.

In design, the hibachi consists of a deep fire bowl, usually rectangular, having a draft door. This is a small vent that can be opened or closed to control the intensity of the heat. Inside the fire bowl is a grate to hold the charcoal. At the top of the hibachi sits a grill. This is the cooking surface, and since it is complete with handles, it can be moved to start the fire, to add fuel, to adjust the firebed, and to clean the hibachi.

COOKING KETTLES

In appearance, the cooking kettle resembles a Dutch oven on legs. Like the brazier, the cooking kettle comes in a multitude of designs.

The cooking kettle, also called a covered barbecue, has adjustable dampers on both the lid and bowl. This controls heat efficiently, so that large cuts of meat and whole poultry cook with a minimum amount of fuel.

Windy days, a complicating factor with the simple brazier, are no problem when using a cooking kettle. Its promoters say that it combines the best features of the broiler, oven, smoker, and grill.

The cooking kettle has a deep fire bowl with a dome-shaped lid. When meat is placed on the grill and the lid put in place, reflected heat in the dome browns the top of the meat, much as your indoor oven does. The temperature within the kettle is controlled by opening or closing dampers. Closing the dampers reduces the heat; opening them increases it.

If there is useable charcoal left when the food is cooked, you can snuff out that inner fire just by closing the dampers. The coals will be ready and waiting to relight next time you cook.

SMOKE OVENS

There are several variations of the smoke oven. One, the *charcoal-water cooker*, is based on an ancient method of cooking meat over water. This cooker, which looks like a miniature version of a space capsule, consists of a dome lid, a grill over a water pan, and a cylindrical base on legs. Some models have a double grill (one above the other) to give twice as much cooking space. Charcoal briquets burn in the fire bowl at the base. After they are glowing, pieces of flavor-producing wood, such as nut or fruitwood, can be added.

An advantage of the charcoal-water cooker is that once it is set up, it can be left without tending for a lengthy smoking period, often several hours, depending upon the food to be cooked.

Similar to the charcoal-water cooker is the *Japanese kamado*. It, too, is a covered barbecue having a barrel-shaped base with a dome lid. The kamado, however, uses no water. Both cookers are an efficient way to handle slow cooking. When using them, all the charcoal that will be needed goes in at the beginning, since the units can't be opened for refills.

No need to worry about wasting charcoal in these smokers. Whatever coals are left at the end of the cooking time will snuff themselves out when the dampers are closed, and can be reused.

Another version is the *Chinese smoker*, a cooker with a chimney located at the end of an enclosed fire bowl. The smoke from the fire travels up the chimney. The food, either suspended on a hook or placed on a rack in the chimney, cooks by the heat from the smoke rather than from the radiant coals.

HIBACHI   COOKING KETTLE

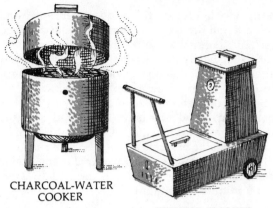

CHARCOAL-WATER
COOKER

CHINESE SMOKER

This type of smoke oven can be portable or permanent, and can be made from a variety of materials such as ceramic, brick, or metal. Here again, it is important to add aromatic wood to the briquets to create a pleasing, smoky flavor.

COOKING WAGONS

The cooking wagon is a rectangular grill available with a variety of features including, as the name suggests, wheels to make it easy to move. Most have grills which can be adjusted to the desired height to control heat. Other embellishments include warming ovens, self-lighters, drawers for tools, and motor-driven rotisseries.

GAS GRILLS

In design, gas grills are similar to charcoal cookers, and come with as many embellishments, or as few, as the buyer wants. The major difference is the source of heat. Gas, either bottled or from a permanent connection to your home's gas line, is less expensive than charcoal.

Gas barbecues use the fuel to heat ceramic or volcanic rock formed to look like coals. These cook the food by radiant energy. Fat dripping onto the simulated coals produces smoke which gives the typical barbecue look and taste to the food. Stronger smoky flavor can be achieved by sprinkling hickory or fruitwood chips over the coals.

Speed is the feature that earns the gas grill its plus marks. In only ten minutes or so, the coals in the gas grill are hot enough to cook with. Charcoal briquets, on the other hand, can take up to an hour, depending upon the weather.

Cleanup is easier with the gas grill, too, as there is no ash, and drips burn away rather quickly. An infrequent scrubbing with a heavy brush keeps the gas grill in apple-pie order; the coals are self-cleaning.

The only precaution with the gas grill is to make sure when the grill is installed that the lowest setting produces about 300 degrees of heat with the top down. The gas cock is the only control on the unit since there are no briquets to remove to lower heat.

Portable gas stoves can be set up on a backyard table or folding stand. These operate on bottled gas and are fine for picnicking and camping as well as backyard use.

Other gas grills range from the covered-kettle type up to fancy, double grill styles, some in ornate cast-iron designs. Many accessories can be purchased to aid in cooking, such as rotisserie baskets and shish kebob rotisseries.

ELECTRIC GRILLS

Shortened time of heating up the grill for cooking: that's a primary advantage of barbecuing with electricity, just as it is with gas. And both electricity and gas are cheaper forms of fuel than charcoal. But to tally total savings, you must consider the initial low cost of the brazier versus the cost of electric or gas models.

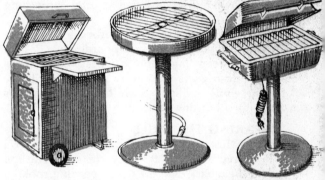

COOKING WAGON   GAS GRILL   ELECTRIC GRILL

In the electric grill an element ignites special lava rock which comes with the unit. When the lava rock is glowing, you can begin grilling. From there on, the techniques are the same as for charcoal and gas grilling.

Electric grilling is another neat form of barbecuing, as the coals are self-cleaning.

FIRE BUILDING
WHERE TO SET UP THE GRILL

For safety's sake, the grill should be located away from brush, dry grass, trees, and bushes. And for your neighbors' sake, locate the grill where smoke won't be a bother. Check the direction of the wind and place the wind screen, if there is one, to shield the coals.

Barbecuing indoors is tricky, as the carbon monoxide it produces is deadly. A small cooker,

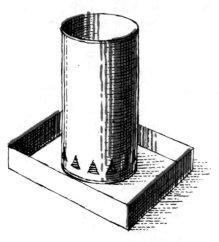

CHIMNEY METHOD OF LIGHTING

like a hibachi, can be placed where there is good ventilation, such as in a fireplace with the draft open.

It's possible to barbecue in the garage if the door is left open. This is usually the last resort of the chef when the skies open up after barbecuing has begun.

City dwellers sometimes barbecue on balconies. Check your lease and city ordinance first. If it's okay, keep flammable material such as rugs and artificial grass well away from the grill. Be careful while grilling. Such freak accidents as dropping a burning coal can be serious.

PREPARING THE GRILL

Line the fire bowl of your briquet-burning grill with heavy duty foil for easy cleanup. The foil reflects heat back onto the food speeding cooking time. Spread a shallow layer of sand, vermiculite, or gravel before adding the briquets. This layer will catch dripping fat to reduce smoking and flaring. It also permits a better draft for the coals.

GETTING THE FIRE GOING

Starting gas and electric grills is a simple matter of turning them on, and allowing ten minutes or so for them to heat. The charcoal grill is another story, and it can take from thirty to sixty minutes to prepare a proper bed of coals, depending upon the weather. If it's cool or windy, allow a full hour.

Some people like the convenience of using an electric starter for charcoal. Of course, this requires an electric outlet in the vicinity of the grill.

Instead of an electric starter, another method is to arrange crushed paper or small pieces of dry kindling wood in the middle of the grill. A few briquets are added, and the kindling lit. When the fire is blazing, more briquets are added.

Liquid Starter

Many people prepare the briquets before igniting with a liquid fire starter. Words of caution: Never use any flammable liquid other than a product made specifically to light charcoal. No gasoline or other combustible liquid, please. And don't sprinkle more starter on an already lighted fire.

Some grill veterans keep a supply of briquets soaking in liquid starter in a covered can, just waiting for barbecue time. A few of these mixed in with regular briquets will speed firing-up.

Pile a few briquets into a pyramid in the firebox of the grill. Douse them with the liquid starter, wait a minute, then light.

Chimney Method of Lighting

A "chimney" made from a tall juice can or two-pound coffee can is another aid to getting the fire started. To make your chimney, remove the ends from the can, and make a row of holes around the bottom, using a punch-type beverage can opener.

Stand the chimney in the firebox of your grill. Put in several fire-starter-soaked briquets if you have them, then add plain briquets. Light at the base of the chimney, through one of the punched holes. Allow the coals to burn fifteen or twenty minutes, remove the chimney with tongs, and rake the coals out into the firebox. Don't start to cook until the fire dies down to glowing coals.

Other Aids to Fire Starting

A candle stub or one-fourth cup of canned heat in a cup made from foil placed in the firebox under the briquets will help to start the fire and keep it going.

FIRE EXPERTISE

Size of Fire

Beginners tend to use more briquets than necessary. Since charcoal is one of the costliest of fuels, this is wasteful. About twenty briquets will grill a few steaks or burgers; use even less if cooking for a twosome. A shallow fire is best for broiling. One that is a little deeper and placed to the rear of the spit works best for rotisserie roasting with a hooded unit.

Judging Readiness of Coals

The fire is ready when the flames die down. In the daytime, the coals will look ash-gray. At night, they'll have a reddish glow.

Just as fingers were made before forks, hands were made before thermometers. To judge whether the fire is hot enough to cook the food, hold your hand at cooking level and count off how many seconds you can comfortably keep it there. This isn't an endurance contest; just a quick check of temperature. If you can keep your hand in place for four seconds, that's about right for food requiring slow cooking. At high heat, you will want to move away in one second. You can dismiss the stopwatch along with the thermometer; just count "one one-thousand, two one-thousand," and so on.

Arranging the Fire

The number of coals and their placement determines cooking heat. A few coals, widely spaced, provide low heat needed for a small cooking job. A generous-sized roast, on the other hand, will take a solid bed of coals. Moving the coals out to form an oval around the food reduces heat; moving the coals in closer increases it.

For Kabobs: Arrange burning coals around sides of the firebox, and in parallel rows through the center area, so that they are spaced between the rows of kabobs above. Use this arrangement for all foods cooked on skewers.

For Steaks: A polka-dot arrangement is recommended, with briquets placed about a half-inch apart in the area under the meat. This produces a more even heat than a haphazard arrangement and reduces flare-ups caused by fat dripping into the firebox.

For Rotisserie Roasting with a Hooded Unit: If spit-roasting on a grill with a reflecting hood, stack the coals slightly to the rear of the spit, extending past the ends of the meat on the spit. A drip pan placed directly under the meat will catch

ROTISSERIE WITH HOODED UNIT

drippings and reduce flaring. Check the position of the drip pan once the juices start to drip.

If the spit is turning properly, that is, away from you at the top and toward you at the bottom, the fat will drip at the front of the firebox and into the pan.

For Rotisserie Roasting with an Open-Top Unit: The "ring of fire" method, attributed to the gypsies, is recommended. Make an oval of glowing coals around and a little bigger than the roast or bird on the spit. The meat should not be directly over the coals. The drip pan should be placed directly under the meat.

Adding More Charcoal

When cooking large cuts of meat or big birds, you may need to add more coals during cooking. Keep some extra briquets at the edge of the grill so you'll have a reserve of hot coals. These can be moved into position with the burning coals and will ignite more quickly than unheated coals.

Avoiding Flare-Ups

Flaring is caused by meat fat dripping onto the coals below. For this reason, it is recommended that you arrange coals around the edges of the meat or between rows of kebobs. Flames are undesirable because they blacken food and can even present a fire hazard.

To douse the flames that do pop up from time to time, keep a laundry sprinkler or water pistol handy. A whisk broom dipped in water will work, too.

Controlling the Heat

The number of coals and their distance from the food determine how quickly the food will cook. If the fire in the grill is too hot, simply raise the grid further up from the heat. If it is not hot enough, lower it.

Placement of coals, as already mentioned, will affect heat, too. Moving coals closer to the food raises heat; moving them out reduces it.

If you find that you have started too many coals, remove some with tongs and douse with water. When dry, they can be used another day.

If your food needs just a small increase in heat, brush the ashes from the tops of the coals. Ash acts as an insulator to hold heat in.

The drafts in your grill are there to control heat, too. Opening them lets more air in, increasing heat. Closing them lowers the heat.

PERFECT FOIL FOR YOUR GRILL SKILL

One of the greatest aids to successful barbecuing is aluminum foil. In fact, it's hard to imagine how those pioneer cooks managed without a roll in the covered wagon.

Nowadays, foil is used in many ways: as a liner for the firebox, to make drip pans, and to wrap packets of food to place in the coals or on the grill, just to name a few.

A *drip pan* is easy to make using aluminum foil; its shape will depend upon the shape of your grill. If yours is rectangular, tear off a piece of heavy-duty foil (eighteen inches wide) large enough for a double thickness the length of the grill. If your grill is round, fashion the drip pan in a half circle. Turn up all four sides to a height of 1½ inches. Fit corners together, miter fashion, and fold the tips inside securely.

The drip pan can be set in place in the grill before or after starting the fire. It can be reused; just empty after each use.

Foil packets can hold a variety of foods, depending upon your menu. A packet of sliced partially precooked potatoes, sliced onions, and a pat of butter, for example, cooks alongside the meat on the grill. It's a no-fuss way of cooking, and cleanup is easy, too. After the meal, just toss away the foil!

Some chefs like to broil on foil, especially with meats such as hamburgers that are tricky to turn on the grill. Tear a "pan" from foil large enough to hold the burgers, and turn up a half-inch edge. Puncture the foil at about two-inch intervals with a fork, then lay on the patties. The holes let the heat up and drippings out so that the burgers broil instead of simmer.

SERVING OUT-OF-DOORS: THE PATIO PANTRY

Chefs who cook outside regularly usually have their own set of tools. These needn't be fancy; they could be kitchen castoffs. But having them all collected and ready can be an enormous help.

Some veteran cooks keep a "tote" of tools in a closet near the back door. This tote could be as unpretentious as a shopping bag, or moving only a step fancier, a plastic bucket. A tray or shallow plastic box might serve the purpose.

Here are a few items outdoor cooks find helpful.

Long-handled tools: meat turner, fork, tongs, spoon
Meat thermometer
Skewers
Asbestos mitts or pot holders
Knife
Sprinkler or water gun for dousing flames
Basting brush
Seasonings: salt, pepper, others of your preference

A hinged broiler to hold hamburgers, hot dogs, or small pieces of fish is handy, but perhaps too large for the tote.

An attractive addition to the patio is a large hanging storage place, made from heavy fabric such as sailcloth. Pockets are stitched horizontally onto the sailcloth, on the order of a shoebag only bigger, with space for each of the cook's tools. This can be hung from hooks on the garage or on any wall near the patio.

The same advice offered for equipment holds true with tools: It's better not to buy a lot before experimenting. Make do with kitchen tools until you find which ones you use most frequently. Then splurge on the beautiful specialized barbecue tools, if you feel like it, or drop a few hints, come Mother's or Father's Day!

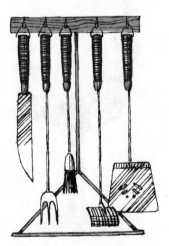

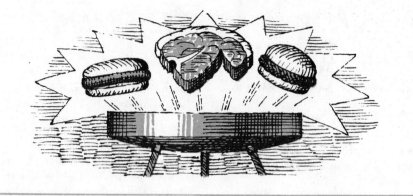

HOT OFF THE GRILL

You can cook up some excitement on the outdoor grill. You needn't stretch the budget doing it either—simply turn loose your imagination. Start with the very foods your family likes best, then add a dash of imagination, using these recipes.

If the chef is a meat-and-potatoes man, keep him happy with meat and potatoes, but give the old combo a new look with the suggestions that follow. Or perhaps the children always vote for hamburgers. Come grill-time, give them Whamburgers—good old ground beef with a new personality.

And so on, down through the list of everybody's favorites. Make them just a little better through the combination of fresh air, charcoal flavor, and your own ingenuity.

Timing of cooking periods will vary with the size of the firebox, degree of heat, amount and direction of wind, and type of grill used. Timings and distances given here are only guides.

Full-Flavored Steak

    2½ tablespoons brown sugar
    1½ tablespoons sugar
     1 tablespoon ground ginger
     1 clove garlic, crushed
    ½ cup soy sauce
     1 tablespoon tarragon vinegar
     3 pounds beefsteak (sirloin, porterhouse,
        T-bone, or rib), cut 1½ inches thick

1. Combine the sugars, ginger, garlic, soy sauce, and vinegar.
2. Put meat into a large shallow dish and pour soy sauce mixture over meat. Allow to marinate at least 30 minutes, basting frequently and turning once or twice.
3. When ready to grill, remove meat from marinade, reserving marinade.
4. Place steak on grill about 3 inches from coals. Brushing frequently with marinade, grill about 6 minutes, or until one side is browned. Turn and grill other side about 6 minutes, or until done. (To test, slit meat near bone and note color of meat.) Serve immediately.

4 to 6 servings

Chuck Steak Teriyaki

    ½ teaspoon salt
     2 teaspoons ground ginger
    ¼ cup soy sauce
     2 cloves garlic, minced
    ½ teaspoon Tabasco
     2 tablespoons molasses
    1½ cups grapefruit juice
    ¼ cup chopped green onion
     1 beef chuck blade steak (4-pounds), 1½
        inches thick

1. Mix salt, ginger, soy sauce, and garlic in a medium bowl. Add Tabasco, molasses, grapefruit juice, and green onion. Put steak into a glass dish and add marinade. Cover; marinate in refrigerator overnight, turning steak occasionally.
2. Remove steak from marinade; place on grill about 5 inches from hot coals. Brush generously with marinade. Grill steak 1½ to 2 hours, basting occasionally and turning steak only once.
3. To serve, cut steak into thin slices.

6 to 8 servings

Grilled Beef Tenderloin

2 envelopes cheese-garlic salad dressing mix
¼ cup salad oil
1 beef tenderloin (3 to 4 pounds)

1. Blend salad dressing mix with oil.
2. Brush tenderloin generously with dressing mixture. Place the meat on a greased grill 4 to 6 inches from the coals.
3. Grill 25 to 35 minutes, or until the tenderloin is done as desired, turning frequently so that the meat cooks and browns evenly on all sides.
4. To serve, cut into thin slices.

6 to 8 servings

Steaks with Herb Butter

¼ cup soft butter or margarine
2 tablespoons chopped green onion
1 tablespoon chopped chives
2 tablespoons chopped parsley
½ teaspoon dill weed
½ teaspoon salt
¼ teaspoon Tabasco
1 tablespoon lemon juice
4 beef rib steaks, 1½ inches thick

1. Combine butter, green onion, chives, parsley, dill, and salt. Add Tabasco and lemon juice gradually, beating until blended.
2. Place steaks on grill about 2 inches from hot coals. Grill steaks about 5 minutes on each side, or until done as desired.
3. Spread steaks with herb butter and serve immediately.

4 servings

Marinated Black Pepper Steak

Purchase a beef sirloin steak, cut 1½ to 2 inches thick. (Allow ¾ to 1 pound per person.) Put steak in a large shallow pan and cover with Steak Marinade; allow to marinate several hours or overnight, turning occasionally. Before grilling, remove steak from marinade and press coarsely crushed peppercorns liberally into both sides of steak. Grill 3 to 4 inches from coals, allowing about 15 minutes for total grilling time; turn once. (Test by slitting meat near bone and noting color of meat.) To serve, cut steak diagonally into thin slices.

Note: The amount of crushed peppercorns used depends entirely on personal taste. As a guide, try 2 teaspoonfuls for each side of a large steak.

Steak Marinade

1 cup red wine vinegar
½ cup salad oil
⅓ cup firmly packed brown sugar
Few drops Tabasco
¼ teaspoon salt
¼ teaspoon marjoram
¼ teaspoon rosemary
¾ cup chopped onion
1 clove garlic, minced

Combine all ingredients in a screw-top jar. Shake well to blend.

About 2 cups marinade

Grilled Sirloin Steak Juliana

1 cup tomato juice
1 cup orange juice
½ cup minced onion
½ cup finely chopped pimento-stuffed olives
2 cloves garlic, crushed
1 tablespoon soy sauce
1 teaspoon salt
1 teaspoon paprika
¼ teaspoon cayenne pepper
Beef sirloin steak, about 2 inches thick (allow ½ to ¾ pound per person)

1. Combine the juices, onion, olives, garlic, and soy sauce; stir in salt, paprika, and cayenne pepper.

Chuck Steak Teriyaki; Steaks with Herb Butter;
Health Burgers; Beef Kabobs

2. Pour sauce over steak in a shallow dish; allow to stand about 1 hour at room temperature, turning occasionally.

3. Transfer steak from sauce to grill and brown quickly on both sides close to hot coals. Continue grilling about 4 inches from coals, basting occasionally with sauce. Allow about 30 minutes total grilling time. (Test by slitting meat near bone and noting color of meat.) To serve, cut steak diagonally into thin slices and serve with remaining heated sauce.

1 steak

Peppered Beef Ribs

  4 **pounds beef rib short ribs, cut in 1-rib pieces**
  2 **cups dill pickle liquid (from quart jar of dill pickles)**
  1 **tablespoon peppercorns**
  ¼ **cup salad oil**
1½ **cups sliced dill pickles**
  2 **tablespoons chopped onion**
  1 **large clove garlic**

1. Put ribs into a shallow dish. Pour pickle liquid over them and marinate several hours or overnight in refrigerator, turning occasionally. Drain well.

2. Put peppercorns into an electric blender container; blend until cracked. Add oil, dill pickles, onion, and garlic; blend until thick and fairly smooth.

3. Place ribs on a preheated gas-fired grill on high heat; brown on all sides. Set a drip pan on briquets under ribs. Brush with pickle-peppercorn mixture, turn heat to low, cover, and cook about 1

hour, or until done as desired; brush ribs occasionally with pickle mixture.

About 4 servings

Barbecued Chuck Steaks

  ½ **cup chopped onion**
  1 **cup ketchup**
  ⅓ **cup red wine vinegar**
  2 **tablespoons brown sugar**
  2 **teaspoons salt**
  ⅛ **teaspoon Tabasco**
  1 **clove garlic, minced**
  1 **bay leaf**
  2 **beef chuck blade steaks, about ¾ inch thick**

1. Combine onion, ketchup, vinegar, brown sugar, salt, Tabasco, garlic, and bay leaf in a saucepan. Bring to boiling; cook slowly 10 minutes, stirring occasionally. Cool.

2. Put steaks into a large baking dish. Pour sauce over steaks and marinate in refrigerator at least 4 hours or overnight.

3. When ready to grill, pour off and reserve marinade. Place steaks on grill over hot coals. Grill about 45 minutes, or until done as desired; occasionally turn and brush steaks with reserved marinade. Prepare Skewered Vegetables, if desired.

4 servings

Skewered Vegetables: Alternate cherry tomatoes, pieces of green pepper, and onions on metal skewers. Brush with marinade for steaks and place on grill to heat the last 5 to 10 minutes steaks are cooking, turning and brushing occasionally.

Herbed Beefsteak

Sprinkle steak (sirloin, porterhouse, T-bone, or rib) generously on both sides with garlic salt. Pour ¼ cup cooking or salad oil into a shallow pan or dish. Put steak into pan and turn to coat with oil. Allow to stand 1 hour, turning occasionally. Grill until meat is done as desired, brushing frequently with Herbed Vinegar.

Herbed Vinegar: Combine ½ cup tarragon vinegar, ½ teaspoon dill weed, crushed, ¼ teaspoon thyme, crushed, and 1 tablespoon finely chopped parsley.

Spit-Roasted Canadian Bacon; Hot Coffee Cake;
Mixed Grill; Pitcher of Sunshine

Rib Steaks, Western Style

1 cup hot bacon drippings
3 tablespoons butter or margarine
⅓ cup lemon juice
3 tablespoons Worcestershire sauce
2 tablespoons ketchup
1 tablespoon paprika
½ cup finely chopped onion
½ clove garlic, crushed
1½ bay leaves
2 teaspoons prepared horseradish
½ teaspoon salt
⅛ teaspoon pepper
4 beef rib steaks, about 1 inch thick (each steak about 1 pound)

1. Mix all ingredients except steaks thoroughly. Pour over steaks and allow to stand about 30 minutes at room temperature for flavors to blend. Remove bay leaves.
2. Lightly grease grill with cooking oil. Place steaks on grill about 3 inches from coals. Grill about 4 minutes, or until first side is browned. Turn with tongs; grill second side about 4 minutes, or until done. (To test, slit meat near bone and note color of meat.) During grilling, baste frequently with the sauce. Serve at once.

4 servings

Hamburger Cups

1 can (8 ounces) tomato sauce
2 tablespoons brown sugar
2 tablespoons dry sherry or vinegar
1 tablespoon Worcestershire sauce
1 tablespoon prepared mustard
½ teaspoon salt
1 egg, slightly beaten
½ cup crumbs from flavored crackers (such as blue cheese, bacon, or onion)
1½ pounds lean ground beef
½ cup dairy sour cream
Blue cheese, crumbled
Sliced green onions

1. Mix thoroughly in a bowl the tomato sauce, brown sugar, wine, Worcestershire sauce, prepared mustard, and salt.
2. Combine egg in a bowl with cracker crumbs, 2 tablespoons of the tomato sauce mixture, and the ground beef. Toss lightly and shape into 6 patties 1 inch thick.

3. Grill 5 inches from hot coals 10 minutes, basting frequently with tomato sauce mixture. Using back of a spoon, form a hollow in each patty. Turn patties and grill about 10 minutes, basting with additional tomato sauce mixture.
4. To serve, arrange patties, hollow side up, on heated platter and fill with the sour cream. Sprinkle with blue cheese and green onion. Spoon Buttered Mushrooms onto platter. Garnish with parsley sprigs. Accompany with Skewered Bread Chunks.

6 servings

Buttered Mushrooms

¾ pound small fresh mushroom caps
2 tablespoons butter or margarine
Salt

1. Put mushrooms onto a large square of heavy-duty aluminum foil. Dot with butter or margarine and sprinkle with salt. Bring ends up and seal tightly, using a drugstore fold and sealing ends.
2. Set package on grill 5 inches from hot coals and cook 25 minutes, turning often.

6 servings

Skewered Bread Chunks

½ cup butter or margarine, softened
1 or 2 cloves garlic, crushed in a garlic press
2 tablespoons minced parsley
1 loaf unsliced French bread, cut in half lengthwise, then crosswise in 2-inch slices
3 tablespoons grated Parmesan cheese

1. Mix butter with garlic and parsley until blended. Spread generously on cut surfaces of bread slices and sprinkle with cheese. Thread onto skewers.
2. Grill 5 inches from hot coals about 5 minutes, or until lightly toasted and hot, turning frequently to brown evenly.

6 servings

Health Burgers

¼ cup toasted wheat germ
3 tablespoons milk
1 tablespoon ketchup
1 teaspoon salt
¼ teaspoon Tabasco
2 tablespoons finely chopped celery
2 tablespoons finely chopped onion
1 pound ground beef round
    Hamburger buns
    Onion rings

1. Mix wheat germ, milk, ketchup, salt, Tabasco, celery, and onion in a bowl. Add meat; mix lightly and thoroughly. Shape into 4 patties.
2. Place on greased grill about 4 inches from hot coals. Grill about 7 minutes on each side, or until meat is done as desired.
3. Serve on buns with onion rings.

4 servings

Avocado Pocketburgers

2 avocados
    Lemon juice
6 slices bacon
6 slices red onion, ⅛ inch thick
    Salt
1½ pounds ground beef chuck
¾ to 1 teaspoon dill weed
    Crumbled blue or grated Parmesan cheese
    (optional)

1. Cut avocados lengthwise into halves; remove seeds and skin. Slice lengthwise; sprinkle with lemon juice.
2. Cook bacon crisp; drain on paper towels. Sauté onion lightly in bacon drippings until crisp-tender, turning once. Drain on paper towels; sprinkle with salt.
3. Mix beef with dill weed and 1½ teaspoons salt; shape on waxed paper into 6 patties about ¼ inch thick.
4. Place an onion slice on one half of each patty, top with 2 avocado slices, and coarsely crumble 1 slice bacon over avocado. Sprinkle with cheese, if desired.
5. Fold other half of patty over filling. Pinch edges together. Cook on grill until browned on one side; turn and finish browning. (Or place on rack in broiler pan; broil 4 inches from heat 2 to 3 minutes on each side or until meat is browned.) Do not overcook.
6. Garnish with remaining avocado slices.

6 servings

Whamburgers

Blend bottled barbecue sauce with lightly seasoned ground beef. Shape into patties. Place on grill about 5 inches from coals. Grill on one side; turn. Spoon additional barbecue sauce over patties and grill until done. Serve on hot toasted buttered buns with additional heated barbecue sauce and assorted relishes.

Double Treat Frank-Burgers

2 pounds ground beef
2 teaspoons salt
    Pepper
2 tablespoons ketchup
6 frankfurters, cut in halves lengthwise
6 strips (½ inch each) Cheddar cheese
3 dill pickles, cut in quarters lengthwise
    Bottled barbecue sauce

1. Lightly toss the ground beef, salt, pepper, and ketchup together. Form into 12 flat patties.
2. Place 2 frankfurter halves, cut side down, on each of 6 patties; place a strip of cheese and two pickle strips between the frankfurter halves. Brush lightly with barbecue sauce. Top with remaining patties and brush with sauce.
3. Place frank-burgers, sauce side down, in a hinged basket broiler. Brush tops with sauce and close broiler. Grill about 3 inches from coals 10 to 15 minutes, frequently turning and brushing with barbecue sauce.

6 servings

Ham Steak Barbecue

   1 smoked ham slice, 1½ inches thick
   1 teaspoon grated grapefruit peel
   1 cup grapefruit juice
   ¼ cup soy sauce
   2 tablespoons salad oil
   2 tablespoons sugar
   1 teaspoon oregano
   ½ teaspoon salt
   ¼ teaspoon pepper
   2 tablespoons chopped parsley
   ¼ cup chopped green onion

1. Put ham slice into a shallow dish. Mix remaining ingredients and pour over ham. Cover and refrigerate 2 hours.

2. Remove ham from marinade and place on grill over hot coals. Grill 25 minutes on one side, basting with marinade; turn and grill 20 minutes longer. Remove from grill and serve with Grapefruit Sauce.

About 6 servings

Grapefruit Sauce

   ½ cup sugar
   2 tablespoons cornstarch
   ¼ teaspoon salt
   ¾ cup water
   1¼ cups grapefruit juice
   1 grapefruit, sectioned and sections halved

1. Mix sugar, cornstarch, and salt in a saucepan. Gradually add water and grapefruit juice, stirring to blend. Cook over low heat, stirring constantly, until mixture thickens and comes to boiling. Simmer 1 minute.

2. Remove from heat and stir in grapefruit pieces.

About 2½ cups sauce

Barbecued Spareribs à la Marinade

   1 package 15-minute meat marinade
   ⅔ cup cold water
   4 pounds pork spareribs

1. Combine meat marinade and water in a large shallow pan; blend thoroughly.

2. Put ribs into marinade. Pierce all surfaces of meat deeply and thoroughly with fork to carry flavor deep down. Marinate only 15 minutes, turning several times. Remove meat from marinade; reserve marinade for basting.

3. Place ribs on grill 4 to 6 inches from hot coals. Cook until crispy brown, about 1 hour, turning and brushing with marinade frequently. Use kitchen shears to cut ribs into pieces for serving.

About 6 servings

Sparerib Appetizers with Hot Nippy Dunks

   5 to 6 pounds meaty pork spareribs, cut in 1-rib pieces
   Bottled barbecue sauce
   Hot Nippy Dunks (see recipes)

1. Partially roast the spareribs in a shallow roasting pan in a 350° F oven about 30 minutes, turning occasionally.

2. Place ribs on the grill, meaty side down, about 3 inches from hot coals; grill slowly. Turn ribs about every 5 minutes, brushing with the barbecue sauce. Grill until meat is deep brown and crisp, about 30 minutes.

3. Accompany ribs with the hot dunks.

Appetizers for 8 to 10

Hot Nippy Dunks

Purple Plum Dunk: Pit the plums from a 17-ounce jar or can; put pitted plums and syrup into container of an electric blender. Add ½ cup bottled barbecue sauce, 2 tablespoons bottled steak sauce, and 1 green onion with green top, cut in pieces. Blend until mixture is puréed. Heat.

Pineapple Dunk: Measure ½ cup bottled barbecue sauce into container of an electric blender. Add ½ cup canned crushed pineapple (do not drain), ½ teaspoon ground ginger, and 1 tablespoon dark brown sugar. Blend until mixture is puréed. Add 1 or 2 strips green pepper to blender just before final blending. Heat.

Apricot Dunk: Combine ½ cup bottled barbecue sauce with ½ cup apricot nectar, 1 tablespoon dark brown sugar, and 1 teaspoon crushed rosemary. Blend all ingredients thoroughly. Heat.

Orange Dunk: Combine ½ cup undiluted frozen orange juice concentrate with ½ cup bottled barbecue sauce, 2 tablespoons dark corn syrup, ½ teaspoon ground ginger, and ½ teaspoon garlic salt. Blend thoroughly. Heat.

Coconut Dunk: Measure ¾ cup bottled barbecue sauce into container of an electric blender. Add ½ cup flaked coconut, 1 tablespoon light molasses, and ¼ teaspoon ground allspice. Blend until coconut is finely chopped. Heat.

Peanut Dunk: Follow recipe for Coconut Dunk. Substitute ¼ cup salted Spanish peanuts for the coconut. Increase the light molasses to 2 tablespoons. Heat.

Spoon stuffing equally onto half of the slices. Top with remaining slices.
4. Brush outside surfaces of meat with oil.
5. Grill slices in a hinged basket broiler or on grill about 6 inches from coals 25 to 30 minutes, turning frequently and brushing with Orange Basting Sauce.

4 generous servings

Stuffed Pork Tenderloin Slices

    8 **pork tenderloin slices**
    4 **slices bacon**
  16 **medium mushrooms, chopped (about 1⅓ cups)**
  ¼ **cup chopped onion**
    2 **tablespoons ketchup**
  ¼ **teaspoon salt**
     Cooking or salad oil
     Orange Basting Sauce, page 54

1. Remove excess fat from meat and flatten to about ¼-inch thickness. Set aside.
2. To make stuffing, cook bacon in a skillet until crisp; drain on absorbent paper, crumble, and set aside. Pour off all but 3 tablespoons bacon fat and add mushrooms and onion to skillet. Cook until mushrooms are lightly browned and onion is soft, stirring frequently. Remove from heat and mix in bacon, ketchup, and salt.
3. Sprinkle meat lightly with additional salt.

Barbecued Pork Chops

    4 **pork chops, 1 inch thick, trimmed**
    1 **can (5½ ounces) tomato juice**
  ¼ **cup cooking oil**
    2 **tablespoons vinegar**
  ¼ **teaspoon Tabasco**
  ¼ **teaspoon Worcestershire sauce**
  ⅛ **teaspoon crushed basil**
    1 **teaspoon vegetable bouquet sauce**

1. Put pork chops into a shallow dish.
2. Mix tomato juice, oil, vinegar, Tabasco, Worcestershire sauce, and basil. Pour over chops. Cover; refrigerate overnight.
3. Remove meat from marinade. Blend 2 tablespoons marinade with bouquet sauce and brush generously over both sides of chops.
4. Set chops on grill 3 to 4 inches from moderately hot coals. Grill 15 minutes on each side, or until done.

4 servings

Marinated Franks

For 1¼ cups marinade, in a shallow dish mix ½ cup soy sauce, ⅓ cup ketchup, ¼ cup salad oil, ¼ cup cider vinegar, 1 teaspoon prepared horseradish, ½ teaspoon dry mustard, and ¼ teaspoon thyme. Cut gashes in frankfurters. Put the frankfurters into marinade and let stand about 3 hours, turning frequently to coat well. Drain and reserve marinade. Put frankfurters into a hinged basket broiler or on grill. Grill about 10 minutes, turning often and basting with reserved marinade.

Bacon-Wrapped Franks

Slit frankfurters almost through lengthwise. Spread cut surfaces with about 1 teaspoon process blue cheese spread. Starting at one end, wrap 1 slice bacon around each frankfurter; secure ends with whole cloves. Put into a hinged basket broiler or on the grill. Grill about 3 inches from coals, turning often, until bacon and frankfurters are lightly browned. (If desired, partially cook bacon before wrapping around franks.)

Lamb Chops Burgundy

  8 lamb loin or rib chops, 1½ to 2 inches thick
  ¼ cup olive oil
  ½ cup Burgundy
  ½ clove garlic, crushed
  ¼ teaspoon salt
  3 peppercorns, crushed
  ½ teaspoon cumin seed, crushed
  ⅔ cup chopped red onion

1. Put chops into a shallow dish; combine remaining ingredients in a screw-top jar; shake to blend.
2. Pour marinade over meat. Cover and set in refrigerator to marinate about 2 hours, turning chops occasionally.
3. Grill chops about 4 inches from coals 16 to 20 minutes, or until meat is browned, turning occasionally and brushing with remaining marinade. (To test, slit meat near bone and note color of meat.)

8 servings

Crunchy Bologna in a Bun

  1 pound bologna, about 2½ inches in diameter (in one piece)
  ⅓ cup bottled barbecue sauce
  1 cup finely crushed potato chips
  Buttered hot dog buns

1. Cut bologna lengthwise into 6 pieces. Coat each piece with the barbecue sauce, then with the potato chips. Allow to stand about 30 minutes to set coating.
2. Grill about 4 inches from coals about 2 minutes on each side, or until coating is browned and the bologna is hot; turn carefully with two forks.
3. Serve in the hot dog buns and, if desired, accompany with crisp carrot and celery sticks, pickles, bowls of potato chips, and an assortment of chilled carbonated beverages.

6 servings

Minted Lamb Chops

  ¼ cup finely chopped mushrooms, lightly browned in butter or margarine
  2 tablespoons crushed fresh mint leaves, or 1 tablespoon dry mint leaves
  ¼ cup firmly packed brown sugar
  1 teaspoon dry mustard
  ½ teaspoon salt
  2 tablespoons wine vinegar
  8 lamb loin or rib chops, 1½ to 2 inches thick

1. Combine mushrooms, mint, brown sugar, dry mustard, salt, and vinegar; toss gently to mix.

2. Grill chops about 4 inches from coals 8 to 10 minutes on one side. Turn chops and spoon mushroom mixture over surface of each; grill second side 8 to 10 minutes, or until done.

8 servings

Ginger-Glazed Lamb Chops with Yams

Season lamb loin double chops with salt, monosodium glutamate, and pepper. Brush with Ginger Glaze and grill 5 to 6 inches from coals 12 to 15 minutes on each side; brush frequently with glaze. Meanwhile, put canned yams into small aluminum foil pans and spoon some of glaze over them. Set on grill; turn and baste with glaze until thoroughly heated.

Ginger Glaze: Mix thoroughly 1 cup ginger marmalade, ¼ cup softened butter or margarine, 2 tablespoons lemon juice, and 1 teaspoon soy sauce.

Mixed Grill

  1 pound lamb, pork, or veal kidneys
  ¼ cup butter or margarine
  1 tablespoon lemon juice
  ½ teaspoon marjoram leaves
 12 large mushroom caps
  3 medium tomatoes, halved
  6 knockwurst
    Salt and pepper
  2 tablespoons chopped parsley

1. Prepare kidneys by slicing in half crosswise and removing fat and connective tissue (if using veal kidneys, cut into chunks and remove fat and connective tissue).
2. Melt butter and add lemon juice and marjoram.
3. Place mushrooms, tomatoes, kidneys, and knockwurst on grill about 5 inches above medium coals. Brush with butter mixture and season with salt and pepper. Turning knockwurst and kidneys occasionally, grill 10 to 15 minutes, or until vegetables are fork tender and knockwurst browned. Kidneys should be slightly pink. Remove from grill and serve, sprinkling parsley over vegetables.

6 servings

Barbecued Ribs

  4 pounds pork loin backribs
  3 cloves garlic, crushed
  ¼ cup cooking or salad oil
  1 cup chopped onion
  1 can (8 ounces) tomato sauce
  ½ cup water
  ¼ cup lemon juice
  3 tablespoons Worcestershire sauce
  ¼ cup firmly packed brown sugar
  1 teaspoon salt
  ¼ teaspoon pepper

1. Rub ribs with crushed garlic; cut into serving-size pieces. Place the ribs in a large shallow pan; set aside.
2. Heat oil in a skillet; add onion and cook until tender, stirring occasionally. Blend in tomato sauce, water, lemon juice, Worcestershire sauce, brown sugar, salt, and pepper; bring to boiling, reduce heat, and simmer 5 minutes.
3. Pour sauce over ribs and marinate 2 hours at room temperature, or overnight in refrigerator.
4. Remove ribs from marinade (reserve for brushing) and put on a grill or in a hinged basket broiler 5 inches from coals. Grill 1 hour or until done, turning and brushing frequently with the marinade.

About 6 servings

Orange-Glazed Pork Loin

- 1 pork loin roast (3 to 5 pounds)
- 3 tablespoons butter
- ½ cup lightly packed brown sugar
- 1 can (6 ounces) frozen orange juice concentrate
- ½ cup water
- 2 teaspoons cornstarch
- 1 cup seeded and halved green grapes

1. Score fat on pork roast at 1-inch intervals. Place roast, fat side up, on grill directly over drip pan prepared from 3 thicknesses of heavy-duty aluminum foil. Insert meat thermometer through fat into very center of the meat. Place cover on kettle-type grill, adjust dampers, and cook at low heat (approximately 350°F) until meat thermometer registers 170°F (allow 20 to 30 minutes per pound).
2. For sauce, heat butter in a 1-quart saucepan. Stir in brown sugar. Add orange concentrate and stir until smooth. Remove ¼ cup sauce and baste roast during last 20 minutes of cooking time.
3. To complete sauce, stir water into cornstarch. Add gradually to remaining orange juice mixture. Cook, stirring constantly until thickened. Cook 8 minutes. Add grapes. Serve hot with pork.

6 to 12 servings

Grilled Turkey Breast Steaks, Chinese Style

- ½ turkey breast (about 2½ pounds)
- 1 teaspoon ground ginger
- 1 teaspoon dry mustard
- ½ teaspoon monosodium glutamate
- ½ cup soy sauce
- ¼ cup dry sherry
- ¼ cup vegetable oil
- 2 tablespoons honey
- 3 cloves garlic, crushed in a garlic press or minced

1. Thaw turkey, if frozen.
2. For marinade, combine ginger, dry mustard, monosodium glutamate, soy sauce, sherry, oil, honey, and garlic in a glass bowl. Cover; set aside at room temperature 24 hours.

3. Skin and bone turkey breast; divide into 6 pieces 1 to 1½ inches thick. Put into a glass dish. Pour soy sauce marinade over turkey; cover and refrigerate several hours or overnight.
4. Remove turkey steaks from marinade and cook on a grill over hot coals, allowing about 8 minutes per side; brush occasionally with marinade.

About 6 servings

Note: If desired, grill a 1-pound piece of turkey breast over hot coals about 45 minutes, turning and brushing frequently with bottled barbecue sauce, until tender.

Turkey Kabobs

Follow recipe for Grilled Turkey Breast Steaks, Chinese Style. Cut the turkey into about 1-inch chunks and refrigerate in the marinade. Thread turkey chunks onto soaked bamboo skewers. Grill, allowing about 7 minutes per side.

12 kabobs

Glazed Whole Chicken on a Grill

- 1 roasting chicken, about 6 pounds
- ½ teaspoon salt
- ¼ teaspoon pepper
- ½ cup soy sauce
- ½ cup ketchup
- ¼ cup light molasses
- ¼ cup dry sherry
- 1 teaspoon garlic powder

1. Sprinkle cavity of chicken with salt and pepper. Tie drumsticks securely to tail. Fasten neck skin to back with skewer. Lock wings behind back.
2. Set chicken in a V-shaped roast holder on rack of a gas-fired grill with an aluminum foil drip pan placed under chicken. Cover grill with hood and cook on low 1 hour.

3. Meanwhile, combine soy sauce, ketchup, molasses, sherry, and garlic powder in a saucepan and heat (on grill, if desired).

4. Brush chicken thoroughly with sauce. Continue cooking, covered, about 30 minutes, or until chicken is tender; brush with sauce about every 10 minutes.

About 6 servings

Glazed Grilled Chicken

Split 2 broiler-fryers (1½ to 2 pounds each) into halves lengthwise. Put chicken halves, cut side down, on a greased grill 3 to 5 inches from coals. Turn and brush with Barbecue Sauce or Currant-Mustard Glaze, page 38, every 5 minutes for even cooking and browning. Grill about 20 minutes, or until chicken tests done. (Chicken is done when meat on thickest part of drumstick cuts easily.)

4 servings

Note: Chicken halves, quarters, or pieces may also be brushed with Tomato Basting Sauce, page 53, Tangy Plum Sauce, page 53, Pineapple Marinade, page 53, or a lemon-flavored butter and placed in a greased hinged basket broiler. Brush frequently with sauce and turn every 5 minutes until chicken tests done.

Barbecue Sauce

  1 **can (8 ounces) tomato sauce**
  1 **can (6 ounces) tomato paste**
  ⅓ **cup chopped onion**
  1 **clove garlic, crushed**
  ¼ **cup firmly packed brown sugar**
  ¼ **cup cider vinegar**
  1 **tablespoon Worcestershire sauce**
  ⅛ **teaspoon Tabasco**
  1 **teaspoon salt**
  ⅛ **teaspoon pepper**
  ½ **teaspoon celery salt**
  ½ **teaspoon dry mustard**
  ½ **teaspoon chili powder**

Combine all ingredients in a heavy saucepan. Bring to boiling, stirring until brown sugar is dissolved. Reduce heat, cover, and simmer about 20 minutes.

About 1½ cups sauce

Note: This sauce keeps well and may be stored in the refrigerator for days before using. Heat before serving.

Apricot-Mustard Glazed Chicken

  ¼ **cup prepared mustard**
  ¼ **cup apricot preserves**
  ¼ **cup vegetable oil**
  2 **broiler-fryer chickens (2½ to 3 pounds each), quartered**

1. Blend mustard, preserves, and oil.
2. Place chickens on grill about 4 inches from hot coals. Grill about 1 hour, or until done; turn occasionally and brush with sauce.

About 8 servings

Saucy Cinnamon Chicken

  ¾ **cup lemon juice**
  ¾ **cup cooking or salad oil**
  6 **tablespoons light corn syrup**
  1 **small clove garlic, crushed**
  1 **tablespoon ground cinnamon**
  1½ **teaspoons curry powder**
  1½ **teaspoons salt**
  2 **broiler-fryers (1½ to 2 pounds each), split lengthwise**

1. Combine the lemon juice, oil, corn syrup, and garlic; stir in cinnamon, curry powder, and salt.
2. Pour mixture over chickens in a shallow pan. Cover and refrigerate several hours or overnight to marinate, turning and basting chickens occasionally.
3. Drain chickens, reserving marinade. Grill about 4 inches from coals, basting frequently with marinade and turning occasionally to brown evenly. Grill about 35 minutes, or until breast meat near wing joint is fork-tender.

4 servings

Chicken Oriental

　　2 broiler-fryers (1 to 1½ pounds each)
　　½ cup soy sauce
　　¼ cup sugar
　　3 drops Tabasco
　1½ teaspoons ground ginger
　　½ teaspoon monosodium glutamate
　　　Few grains paprika
　　1 clove garlic, crushed
　　　Melted butter or margarine

1. Clean, rinse, and dry chickens. Split each chicken in half lengthwise. (If chickens are frozen, thaw according to directions on package.) Crack joints of drumsticks, thighs, and wings so chicken can be kept flat during grilling.
2. Combine in a large shallow dish the soy sauce, sugar, Tabasco, ginger, monosodium glutamate, paprika, and garlic. Add chicken to soy sauce marinade; cover and marinate about 3 hours, turning occasionally.
3. Drain and reserve marinade for basting. Place chicken halves on greased grill or in a greased hinged basket broiler. Brush with melted butter. Grill, cut side down, about 3 inches from coals. Turn every 5 minutes to brown and cook evenly. Brush frequently with reserved marinade.
4. Grill about 20 minutes, or until chickens test done. (Meat on thickest part of drumstick should cut easily and show no pink.)

4 servings

Grilled Chicken

　　Lemon Basting Sauce
　3 **broiler chickens (1½ pounds each), cut in halves**

1. Clean, rinse, and pat the chickens dry with absorbent paper.
2. Place chickens, cut side down, on greased grill or in a greased hinged basket broiler 6 inches from coals. Grill, turning and brushing frequently with sauce, until tender.

6 servings

Lemon Basting Sauce: Melt ¾ cup butter in a small heavy saucepan. Stir in ⅓ to ½ cup lemon juice, ½ cup hot water, few drops Tabasco, and a mixture of 2 teaspoons paprika, 1 teaspoon sugar, 1 teaspoon salt, ½ teaspoon black pepper, and ¼ teaspoon dry mustard. Mix until thoroughly blended.

About 2 cups sauce

Ginger Chicken

　1⅓ cups honey
　　½ cup currant jelly
　　½ cup finely chopped preserved ginger
　　6 cloves garlic, crushed in a garlic press
　　1 tablespoon salt
　　¼ teaspoon Tabasco
　　2 broiler-fryer chickens (2¼ to 2½ pounds each), quartered

1. Combine first 6 ingredients in a saucepan; heat, stirring occasionally, until jelly is melted. Remove from heat.
2. Place chicken quarters on greased grill. Brush with sauce. Grill 8 inches from source of heat about 30 minutes, turning and brushing with sauce every 5 minutes until chicken tests done.

8 servings

Note: If this sauce is made in advance and stored, the flavors will intensify.

Grilled Trout with Herb-Lemon Butter

　3 or 4 trout (about 10 ounces each)
　¼ cup butter or margarine
　2 tablespoons lemon juice
　½ teaspoon chervil
　¼ teaspoon tarragon leaves, crushed

1. Place trout on a greased grill 3 inches from coals; grill 5 minutes on each side, or until done.
2. Meanwhile, heat butter, lemon juice, and

herbs together in a small saucepan on grill until butter is melted. Stir until blended.

3. Serve trout with French Fried Potatoes, drizzling lemon butter over the trout and, if desired, over the potatoes.

3 or 4 servings

French Fried Potatoes

2 (9-ounce) packages or 1 (1-pound) package frozen French fried potatoes; do not thaw
1 teaspoon salt

1. Cut two 18×14-inch pieces of aluminum foil. Turn up all edges 1½ inches; miter corners securely and fold tips against sides. Puncture bottom of pan at frequent intervals to form holes ⅛ to ¼ inch in diameter.

2. Spread the potatoes one layer deep in pan and sprinkle with the salt. Set on grill 2 to 3 inches from coals (mound coals slightly to concentrate heat). Grill until potatoes are golden brown; occasionally shake pan and turn potatoes to insure even browning.

3 or 4 servings

Grilled Trout

6 cleaned fresh trout (about 5 to 6 ounces each)
⅔ cup olive oil
¼ cup lemon juice
2 tablespoons water
2 tablespoons grated onion
2 tablespoons minced parsley
2 teaspoons salt
½ teaspoon black pepper
1 teaspoon curry powder
½ teaspoon celery flakes
½ teaspoon tarragon

1. Remove heads and fins from trout, if desired; rinse trout under cold running water and pat dry with absorbent paper. Put into a shallow dish.

2. Combine remaining ingredients in a screw-top jar. Shake well to blend. Pour over trout, cover, and set in refrigerator to marinate at least 2 hours, turning occasionally.

3. Drain and reserve marinade. Put trout on greased grill or in a greased hinged basket broiler; brush with marinade. Grill 3 inches from coals about 4 minutes; turn, brush with marinade, and grill second side about 4 minutes, or until fish flakes easily. Serve immediately.

6 servings

Note: Other fresh-water fish may be prepared this way.

Grilled Fresh Pineapple Slices

Cut a small fresh pineapple into slices, ¾ to 1 inch thick. Set on grill over hot coals and heat until lightly browned, about 5 minutes per side.

Italian Style Halibut Steaks

2 pounds halibut steaks or other fish steaks, fresh or frozen
2 cups Italian salad dressing
2 tablespoons lemon juice
2 teaspoons salt
¼ teaspoon pepper
Paprika

1. Thaw fish, if frozen. Cut into serving-size portions and place in a single layer in a shallow baking dish.

2. Combine salad dressing, lemon juice, salt, and pepper; pour over fish and let stand 30 minutes, turning once.

3. Remove fish, reserving marinade for basting; place fish on a greased grill or in a well-greased hinged basket broiler. Sprinkle fish with paprika. Cook about 4 inches from moderately hot coals about 8 minutes. Baste with sauce and sprinkle with paprika. Turn and cook about 10 minutes, or until fish flakes easily when tested with a fork.

About 6 servings

Rock Lobster Tails with Orange-Butter Sauce

    1 can (6 ounces) frozen orange juice concentrate, undiluted
    ¼ cup lemon juice
    ½ teaspoon dry mustard
    ¼ teaspoon rosemary
    ½ teaspoon celery salt
    ½ teaspoon onion powder
    ½ teaspoon salt
    ¼ teaspoon Angostura bitters
    ½ cup butter or margarine
    12 frozen South African rock lobster tails (2 packages, 1½ pounds each)

1. For sauce, combine all ingredients except butter and lobster in a saucepan; heat slowly, stirring constantly, until mixture comes to a boil; boil 1 minute.
2. When ready to grill, melt butter in a small saucepan over fire; add sauce, stirring to blend thoroughly; use to brush rock lobster tails during grilling and serve remaining sauce for dipping.
3. Let frozen rock lobster tails thaw gradually; when ready to cook, slit thin underside membrane down center and peel open; insert tails on long skewers. (If tails are cooked flat on grill, prevent curling by bending tails backward to crack sharply in several places.)
4. Grill tails, shell side down, about 4 inches from coals 5 minutes, brushing occasionally with butter sauce; turn tails and grill 5 minutes longer, or until meat is opaque and creamy white.
5. Serve with remaining sauce.

8 servings

Rock Lobster Tails Superb

    4 frozen South African rock lobster tails (8 ounces each)
    Boiling salted water
    ½ cup cooking or salad oil
    2 tablespoons soy sauce
    1 tablespoon minced onion
    1 teaspoon salt
    ½ teaspoon pepper
    1 teaspoon dry mustard
    1 teaspoon ground ginger
    1 clove garlic, crushed

1. Drop lobster tails into boiling salted water to cover. Bring to boiling, lower heat, and simmer about 5 minutes, or until just tender and opaque. Drain and cool.
2. Using scissors, cut through center of bony membrane and remove meat from shell in one piece.
3. Combine remaining ingredients for marinade; pour over lobster tails in a shallow dish; cover and refrigerate about 3 hours, turning occasionally.
4. Remove lobster tails from marinade and thread each one on an 8-inch skewer. Grill about 3 inches from coals until light golden in color and thoroughly heated, brushing frequently with marinade.

4 servings

Grilled Rock Lobster Tails

    6 frozen South African rock lobster tails, thawed
    ¾ cup pineapple juice
    ½ cup packed brown sugar
    ¼ cup cider vinegar
    2½ teaspoons dry mustard

1. Cut underside membrane of lobster tails around edges and remove. Insert skewers lengthwise through meat to keep tails flat during cooking.
2. Place on grill about 4 inches from coals, flesh side down, 3 to 5 minutes. Turn, brush meat with a mixture of pineapple juice and remaining ingredients, and continue grilling until meat is opaque and tender. Brush meat several times during

cooking and just before serving. Serve with remaining sauce and, if desired, lemon wedges.

6 servings

Note: Butter Sauce, page 53, may be substituted for the pineapple mixture.

Grilled Lobster

1 live lobster (about 1½ pounds)
Tabasco Butter (page 54; see *Note*)

1. Purchase a lobster for each serving. Live lobsters may be killed and dressed for cooking at the market. If prepared at home, place the lobster on a cutting board with back or smooth shell up. Hold a towel firmly over the head and claws. Kill by quickly inserting the point of a sharp heavy knife into the center of the small cross showing on the back of the head. Without removing knife, quickly bear down heavily, cutting through entire length of the body and tail. Split the halves apart and remove the stomach, a small sac which lies in the head, and the spongy lungs which lie between meat and shell. Also remove the dark intestinal line running through the center of the body. Crack large claws with a nutcracker or mallet.

2. Brush meat with Tabasco Butter. Place shell side down on grill about 5 inches from coals. Grill about 20 minutes, or until shell is browned. Baste frequently with butter. Serve in shell with remaining butter.

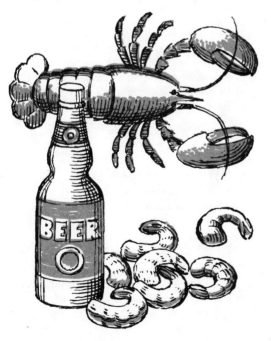

Grilled Shrimp in Beer

   2 pounds raw medium shrimp, shelled
   2 cups beer
   1 tablespoon chopped chives or 2 teaspoons
      chopped scallion tops
   1 tablespoon chopped fresh parsley
   2 teaspoons dry mustard
  ⅛ teaspoon garlic powder
   1 teaspoon salt
  ½ teaspoon freshly ground black pepper

1. Blend the beer and other ingredients, except shrimp, in a large bowl. Add shrimp and refrigerate overnight; stir occasionally.

2. Drain the shrimp and grill them in a hinged basket broiler or on a grill about 3 inches from coals about 2 minutes on each side. Serve immediately.

4 to 6 servings

Grilled Shrimp in Shells

   2 pounds jumbo shrimp or prawns, fresh or
      thawed frozen (about 24)
   1 cup olive oil
  ½ cup lemon juice
   2 tablespoons soy sauce
  ½ teaspoon salt
   1 large clove garlic, crushed
   2 tablespoons chopped parsley
  ½ teaspoon thyme, crushed
  ½ teaspoon marjoram, crushed
  ½ teaspoon celery seed

1. Using scissors, cut through shell at the back of each raw shrimp; remove the black vein. Wash shrimp with shells thoroughly; drain on absorbent paper. Put the shrimp into a large bowl.

2. Combine remaining ingredients; mix well and pour over shrimp. Cover and refrigerate at least 2 hours, turning shrimp several times.

3. Arrange the shrimp in a hinged basket broiler. Grill about 3 inches from coals until shells are slightly charred. Turn broiler and grill shrimp several minutes longer. Serve immediately.

About 6 servings

Note: If desired, substitute 1 tablespoon chopped onion for garlic. Omit thyme, marjoram, and celery seed. Add 4 teaspoons crushed tarragon, ½ teaspoon chervil, and ¼ teaspoon basil.

HOT OFF THE GRILL AND
ON THE SKEWER

Beef Kabobs

- 3 tablespoons brown sugar
- ¼ teaspoon dry mustard
- 1 cup soy sauce
- ½ cup water
- 3 tablespoons dry sherry
- ¼ teaspoon Tabasco
- 1 tablespoon grated onion
- 1 clove garlic, minced
- 2 pounds beef sirloin, cut in 1-inch cubes
  Zucchini, cut in 1-inch slices
  Cherry tomatoes
  Medium mushrooms, cleaned

1. Mix brown sugar, mustard, soy sauce, water, sherry, Tabasco, onion, and garlic in a bowl. Add meat, cover, and marinate at room temperature 1 hour. Remove meat and reserve marinade.
2. Alternate cubes of meat, zucchini, tomatoes, and mushrooms on skewers.
3. Place kabobs on grill about 5 inches from hot coals. Brush generously with marinade. Grill 7 minutes; turn and grill 7 minutes, or until meat is done as desired.

About 6 servings

Ginger Beef

- 2 pounds beef (tenderloin, sirloin, or rib), boneless, cut 1¼ inches thick
- ½ cup soy sauce
- 3 tablespoons honey
- 1 clove garlic, minced
- 2 tablespoons finely chopped crystallized ginger

1. Slice meat across grain into ¼-inch strips.
2. Thoroughly mix the soy sauce, honey, garlic, and ginger; add the meat strips and toss to coat evenly. Marinate at least 30 minutes, turning meat occasionally.
3. Remove meat strips from marinade. Thread each strip onto a bamboo skewer (soak skewers in water before using). Grill 3 inches from coals about 3 minutes, turning once and brushing with marinade. (Meat should be rare.)

About 6 servings

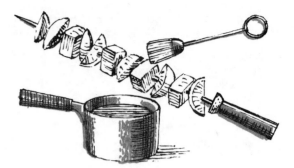

Glazed Beef-Fruit Kabob Duo

- 3 pounds beef sirloin, rib, or tenderloin, boneless, cut in 1½-inch cubes
  Spicy Apricot-Lime Sauce
  Glazed Fruit Kabobs

1. Thread beef cubes onto eight 5-inch skewers, separating pieces slightly. Brush with Spicy Apricot-Lime Sauce. Place on a greased grill and cook 4 to 5 inches from coals, turning and brushing frequently with the sauce until meat is the desired degree of doneness, 12 to 15 minutes.
2. Arrange beef and fruit kabobs on fluffy cooked rice, if desired. Serve immediately with the remaining hot sauce.

8 servings

Glazed Fruit Kabobs

Thread alternately onto eight 4-inch skewers, 16 large orange wedges (use 4 large oranges, peeled), 16 lime slices (2 large limes, cut in ¼-inch slices), and 16 honeydew melon slices, 2¾ inches each. Brush with Spicy Apricot-Lime Sauce; and grill or broil 4 to 5 inches from source of heat about 10 minutes, turning and brushing frequently with the sauce until fruit is heated and well glazed.

Spicy Apricot-Lime Sauce
- 1 cup apricot preserves
- ½ cup light corn syrup
- ½ cup butter
- ¼ cup lime juice
- 1 teaspoon ground cinnamon
- ¼ teaspoon ground cloves

Combine all ingredients in a saucepan. Stirring occasionally, bring slowly to simmering and cook until slightly thicker, about 10 minutes.

2 cups sauce

Beef Kabobs with Oriental Sauce

    ¾ cup cooking or salad oil
    ¼ cup soy sauce
    3 tablespoons honey
    2 tablespoons cider vinegar
    1½ teaspoons ground ginger
    1½ teaspoons garlic powder
    1½ teaspoons finely chopped green onion
    1½ pounds beef loin sirloin steak, boneless, cut in 1½-inch cubes

1. Combine oil, soy sauce, honey, vinegar, ground ginger, garlic powder, and chopped green onion in a large shallow dish. Add the meat cubes; turn until pieces are coated. Set in refrigerator to marinate for at least 4 hours, turning several times.
2. Remove meat from marinade with a slotted spoon and drain. Reserve marinade for basting.
3. Thread three meat cubes onto each 6-inch skewer. Place meat cubes close together for rare; separate cubes slightly for well done.
4. Grill kabobs on a greased grill about 3 inches from coals, turning often for even browning. Baste frequently with marinade. Grilling period ranges from 10 to 20 minutes, or until meat is done to the desired stage. (Test by cutting a slit in meat and noting internal color.)

About 4 servings

Barbecued Bologna Roll

    1 bologna roll (4 pounds)
    1½ tablespoons prepared mustard
    1½ teaspoons brown sugar
    1 teaspoon prepared horseradish
    1 cup chili sauce
    3 tablespoons cider vinegar

1. Score bologna roll on one side, making cuts ½ to 1 inch deep and 1 inch apart. Secure roll on a long skewer.
2. Mix mustard, brown sugar, and horseradish. Spread into cuts.
3. Place roll directly on grill about 3 inches from coals. Baste well with a mixture of chili sauce and vinegar. Turning frequently, grill 15 to 20 minutes or until roll is thoroughly heated and browned.
4. Remove skewer and slice meat.

16 servings

Ham 'n' Pickle Kabobs

    1 jar (10 ounces, about 1 cup) currant jelly
    ⅓ cup prepared mustard
    2 tablespoons light corn syrup
    Cooked ham (about 1½ pounds), cut in 1-inch cubes
    8 to 10 canned peach halves, each cut in 3 wedges
    Pickle slices

1. Melt jelly in a saucepan. Blend in mustard and corn syrup until well blended; boil 2 minutes.
2. Stir in ham cubes; reduce heat and simmer, covered, 20 minutes. Gently stir in peaches and pickle slices; cover and heat 10 minutes. Drain sauce from ham, peaches, and pickles and reserve for brushing on kabobs.
3. Alternately thread ham cubes, pairs of pickle slices, and peach wedges onto skewers, starting and ending with ham. Brush kabobs with sauce.
4. Grill about 4 inches from coals until ham is thoroughly browned, turning and brushing frequently with sauce; allow about 30 minutes grilling time.

About 8 kabobs

Quickie Kabobs

Allowing ¼ pound meat per serving, cut canned luncheon meat or bologna into 1- to 1½-inch cubes; cut green pepper and bacon into 1- to 1½-inch pieces. Alternately thread onto skewers along with pitted olives. Grill on greased grill about 3 inches from coals about 5 minutes, turning and brushing constantly with your favorite salad dressing (bottled or prepared from a mix) or a bottled barbecue sauce.

Help-Yourself Appetizer Kabobs

Arrange a Lazy Susan or tray with individual bowls of canned Vienna sausage, cut in halves, thick slices of banana (having green-tipped peel), pineapple chunks, pitted large ripe olives, canned green chilies, cut in large pieces, and bottled sweet-and-sour sauce. Spear morsels (your choice) on a 6-inch skewer, coat generously with the sauce, and grill 2 to 3 inches from coals until sauce is bubbly and tidbits begin to brown.

Frank and Vegetable Kabobs

6 frankfurters, cut in 1½-inch pieces
1 large green pepper, cut in 1½-inch squares
12 small cooked potatoes (use canned, if desired)
6 small cooked onions (use canned, if desired)
Favorite bottled barbecue sauce

1. Using 6 long skewers, thread on each: 1 piece meat, 1 square green pepper, 1 potato, and 1 onion; repeat to fill the skewer.
2. Brush kabobs generously with melted butter or margarine and then with barbecue sauce. Place on the grill about 4 inches from hot coals and cook until franks and vegetables are thoroughly heated and lightly browned, turning occasionally.

About 6 servings

Frankfurter Kabobs

12 frankfurters, each cut in 3 or 4 pieces
12 whole mushrooms, cleaned
3 medium tomatoes, cut in quarters or eighths
1 cup Basic Molasses Barbecue Sauce (see recipe)
1 tablespoon prepared mustard
1 to 2 tablespoons pineapple syrup (optional)

1. Thread franks, mushrooms, and tomato pieces onto 8- to 10-inch skewers.

2. Combine sauce, mustard, and pineapple syrup, if used. Mix well and brush generously over kabobs.
3. Cook 5 to 6 inches above the hot coals, 3 to 4 minutes on each side; brush with the sauce several times during cooking.

6 kabobs

Vegetable Kabobs

Follow recipe for Frankfurter Kabobs except: Insert on 6 skewers the following:
½-inch thick slices yellow squash or 1-inch thick slices zucchini
12 cherry tomatoes
1-inch strips green pepper (using 2 peppers)
1-inch cubes unpared eggplant (using 1 small eggplant)
Small cooked white onions (16-ounce can, drained)
12 whole mushrooms, cleaned

Omit prepared mustard and add ½ cup chili sauce. Increase grilling time to 5 minutes on each side.

Shrimp Kabobs

Follow recipe for Frankfurter Kabobs except: Insert on 6 skewers the following:
Raw shrimp (about 2 pounds), shelled (leaving on tails) and deveined
1-inch strips green pepper (using 2 peppers)
Small cooked white onions (16-ounce can, drained)
12 whole mushrooms, cleaned
12 large pimento-stuffed olives
12 large pitted ripe olives

Omit prepared mustard. Add 1 tablespoon prepared horseradish. Grill kabobs 5 minutes on each side.

Basic Molasses Barbecue Sauce

¼ cup cornstarch
4 cups lemon juice
2 cups cooking oil
1 jar (12 ounces) light or dark molasses
¼ cup salt
1 tablespoon black pepper
6 bay leaves, broken in pieces
3 cloves garlic, minced

1. Combine cornstarch and lemon juice in a saucepan. Cook and stir over low heat until mixture bubbles and thickens. Cool.
2. Using rotary or electric beater, beat in remain-

ing ingredients until thoroughly blended and thickened.

3. Store in refrigerator until needed.

About 2 quarts sauce

Spicy Grilled Chicken

½ cup lime juice
¼ cup soy sauce
½ teaspoon salt
¼ teaspoon pepper
1 teaspoon ground ginger
1 tablespoon ground coriander
1 clove garlic, minced
½ cup cooking oil
3 ready-to-cook broiler-fryer chickens, about 2 pounds each, cut into halves
1 fresh pineapple, cut into 1-inch-thick slices and quartered

1. In a screw-top jar, shake lime juice and soy sauce; add dry seasonings and shake vigorously. Then add garlic and oil and shake. Set aside.
2. Crack thigh and wing joints of chicken so they will be flat.
3. Put chicken halves and pineapple in a shallow pan. Shake marinade and pour over all. Cover and marinate at least 2 hours, turning and basting occasionally.
4. Thread chicken halves and pineapple onto long skewers. Brush with marinade. Grill 4 inches from hot coals. Turn every 5 minutes, brushing with marinade. Grill 40 minutes, or until chicken tests done (meat on thickest part of drumstick will cut easily).
5. Accompany grilled chicken and pineapple, if desired, with chutney, salted peanuts, cherry tomatoes, banana chunks, and soy sauce for dipping.

6 servings

Rumaki

1 package (8 ounces) frozen chicken livers
1 pound raw small shrimp, shelled
1 small can water chestnuts, drained
10 to 12 slices bacon, halved lengthwise

1. Thaw chicken livers and cut each one in half. If shrimp are overly large, cut them in half. Cut water chestnuts in half. Wrap a piece of chicken liver, one of shrimp, and one of water chestnut as tightly as possible with one or two strips of bacon, and secure with a cocktail pick.
2. Cook over charcoal until the bacon is done, 6 to 8 minutes. Serve immediately.

6 to 8 servings

Shish Kabobs

1½ pounds lamb (loin, leg, or shoulder), boneless, cut in 1½-inch cubes
1½ cups olive oil
3 tablespoons lemon juice
12 large mushroom caps
Bacon slices
6 small whole cooked potatoes
6 small whole cooked onions
Melted butter or margarine
6 plum tomatoes
2 teaspoons salt
½ teaspoon monosodium glutamate
¼ teaspoon black pepper

1. Put meat cubes into a shallow dish. Pour a mixture of olive oil and lemon juice over them. Cover and marinate 1 hour or longer in refrigerator, turning pieces occasionally. Drain.
2. Wrap each mushroom cap with bacon. Alternately thread lamb cubes, mushroom caps, potatoes, and onions on 6 skewers. Brush pieces with melted butter.
3. Grill about 3 inches from the coals 10 to 12 minutes, or until lightly browned; turn frequently for even browning and brush frequently with melted butter. Put a plum tomato on the end of each skewer; grill 3 to 5 minutes longer. Season kabobs with a mixture of remaining ingredients.

6 kabobs

Orange-Glazed Pork Loin; Kettle Patio Potatoes;
Sour Cream Slaw; Vegetable Medley

Shoulder Lamb Chops en Brochette

6 lamb shoulder arm chops, 1½ to 2 inches
    thick (about 3½ pounds)
  Garlic clove, halved
12 shelled Brazil nuts
18 tomato wedges or cherry tomatoes
12 large mushrooms
1½ cups bottled Italian dressing
6 slices bacon, halved

1. To keep lamb chops flat, slash fat at intervals.
Rub chops with garlic. Put into a shallow dish
along with nuts, tomatoes, and mushrooms. Pour
dressing over all and marinate several hours,
turning occasionally.
2. Remove chops from marinade and thread onto
long skewers. Brush with marinade.
3. Grill chops about 4 inches from coals 22 to 30
minutes, turning several times and brushing frequently with marinade.
4. Wrap nuts in bacon and thread alternately with
tomatoes and mushrooms onto 3 long skewers.
Brush with marinade.
5. Grill vegetable kabobs about 10 minutes, turning and brushing frequently with the marinade.

6 servings

Shoulder Lamb Chops and Vegetables

6 lamb shoulder arm chops, cut about 1½
    inches thick
¼ cup lemon juice
1 clove garlic, minced
¼ teaspoon marjoram leaves, crushed
¼ teaspoon rosemary leaves, crushed
¼ teaspoon tarragon leaves, crushed
¼ teaspoon ground thyme
⅛ teaspoon onion powder
¾ cup cooking or salad oil
  Lemon pepper marinade
1 package (10 ounces) frozen cauliflower,
    partially cooked and drained
  Green pepper squares (about 1½ inches)
  Tomato wedges

1. Put lamb chops into a large shallow dish.

2. Combine lemon juice, garlic, herbs, onion
powder, and oil; mix well. Pour over lamb and
marinate in refrigerator several hours, turning
chops over occasionally.
3. Remove chops from marinade (reserve for
brushing) and thread 2 chops on each of 3 long
skewers. Put on a hot grill about 4 inches from
coals. During grilling, turn chops frequently and
brush with marinade. Cook about 18 minutes, or
until done. (To test, slit meat near bone and note
the color of the meat.) Season with lemon pepper
marinade.
4. Meanwhile, thread vegetable pieces alternately on long skewers. Brush generously with marinade. Grill until done as desired, turning and
brushing with marinade.
5. When meat and vegetables are done, remove
from skewers to plates.

6 servings

Vegetables on Skewers

1 can (16 ounces) artichoke hearts, drained
1 jar (16 ounces) small white onions,
    drained (not cocktail size)
½ pound medium mushrooms, stems
    removed
12 small whole tomatoes
2 medium green peppers, cut in 1-inch
    squares
¾ cup salad oil
¼ cup cider vinegar
1½ to 2 teaspoons salt
⅛ teaspoon black pepper
1 clove garlic, split

1. Put vegetables in a bowl. Mix remaining ingredients and pour over them. Cover and marinate 2

hours in refrigerator, turning occasionally. Drain vegetables and reserve marinade.

2. Thread vegetables on each of 12 (10-inch) skewers in this order: mushroom cap, artichoke heart, green pepper square, tomato, onion, green pepper square, and mushroom cap.

3. Turning and brushing frequently with the reserved marinade, grill kabobs about 6 inches from coals about 10 minutes, or until thoroughly heated.

12 kabobs

Lamb Kabobs

1½ pounds lamb (loin, leg, or shoulder),
    boneless, cut in 1½-inch cubes
½ cup cider vinegar
⅓ cup olive oil
¼ cup corn syrup
2 tablespoons piccalilli
1 tablespoon dry mustard
1 teaspoon salt
½ teaspoon pepper
2 tablespoons capers

1. Put lamb cubes into a shallow dish. Pour a mixture of vinegar and remaining ingredients over them. Marinate at least 6 hours, turning pieces occasionally. Drain the meat, reserving marinade.

2. Thread meat cubes onto skewers. Place rather close together for rare meat, or separate slightly for well done.

3. Place on grill about 3 inches from coals and cook 15 to 20 minutes, or until tender and browned, frequently turning and brushing the meat with marinade.

About 4 servings

Soy Marinated Lamb Kabobs

½ cup soy sauce
1 clove garlic, crushed
1 teaspoon chopped candied ginger
3 tablespoons sugar
1½ pounds lamb (leg or shoulder), boneless,
    cut in 1½-inch cubes
Mushroom caps
Green pepper squares (1 inch)
Pimento-stuffed olives

1. Combine the soy sauce, garlic, ginger, and sugar in a shallow dish. Add the meat cubes and

turn until pieces are coated. Refrigerate at least 6 hours, turning several times.

2. Remove meat from marinade with a slotted spoon and drain; reserve marinade for basting.

3. Alternately thread onto 4 (16-inch) skewers mushrooms, lamb, green pepper, and olives, ending each skewer with a mushroom and olive.

4. Basting generously and frequently, grill kabobs on a greased grill about 3 inches from coals about 20 minutes, or until meat is tender and rich brown.

About 4 servings

Grilled Shrimp Appetizers

Shell fresh shrimp, leaving tails; devein and rinse under running cold water; put into a large bowl. Partially cover with bottled Italian salad dressing; cover bowl and refrigerate at least 2 hours, turning shrimp several times. Drain shrimp, reserving marinade. Thread onto metal or bamboo skewers (soak bamboo skewers in water before using): shrimp, cherry tomatoes, green pepper squares, and avocado pieces. Grill 3 inches from coals about 3 minutes, or until shrimp are done, turning and brushing with marinade.

Shrimp Skewers

36 raw medium shrimp, shelled
¾ cup cooking sherry
¾ cup soy sauce
1 tablespoon sugar
⅛ teaspoon ground ginger

1. Mix sherry, soy sauce, sugar, and ground ginger in a saucepan; bring rapidly to boiling. Remove from heat and cool to room temperature.

2. Wash shelled raw shrimp and thread them sideways, heads doubled up against the tails, onto 9-inch metal or bamboo skewers. Use 4 per skewer, placing shrimp near center of each. Refrigerate at least 1 hour.

3. Cook on a charcoal brazier or at the table on a hibachi, brushing with sauce and turning the shrimp often until they are glazed, about 10 to 12 minutes. Serve at once.

4 to 6 servings

Scallop Kabobs

1 pound scallops, fresh or thawed frozen
¼ cup olive oil or other cooking oil
1 small clove garlic, crushed
¼ cup lemon juice
¼ cup finely chopped parsley
¼ cup soy sauce
½ teaspoon salt
  Freshly ground pepper
1 can (13 to 13½ ounces) pineapple chunks,
    drained
1 can (4 ounces) button mushrooms, drained
  Green pepper squares (about 1 inch)
12 slices bacon

1. Rinse scallops with cold water to remove any pieces of shell; drain on absorbent paper. Cut large scallops into smaller pieces.
2. Combine oil, garlic, lemon juice, parsley, soy sauce, salt, and pepper to taste in a large bowl. Mix thoroughly and add the scallops, pineapple chunks, mushrooms, and green pepper pieces. Toss to coat ingredients with the marinade. Set aside at least 30 minutes, tossing several times.
3. Meanwhile, panbroil the bacon until cooked but still soft. Halve the slices.
4. Using long, thin skewers, thread each with a scallop, pineapple chunk, mushroom cap, green pepper piece, and bacon piece; repeat to fill skewer.
5. Brush kabobs with some of the leftover marinade and place on grill about 4 inches from the hot coals. Cook until bacon is crisp and browned, 10 to 12 minutes. Turn kabobs several times while cooking and brush with the marinade.

About 6 servings

Shrimp Satay

1 pound raw shrimp, shelled
1 cup coconut milk (see note)
1 teaspoon salt
⅛ teaspoon ground ginger
1 tablespoon brown sugar
½ teaspoon ground dried chili peppers
1 tablespoon soy sauce
1 tablespoon lime juice

1. Combine all of the ingredients except the shrimp in a shallow bowl. At room temperature, marinate shrimp in this satay (or sate) sauce for 30 minutes, turning shrimp frequently.
2. Remove shrimp from the marinade with a slotted spoon and thread them, head to tail, onto bamboo or metal skewers, 3 or 4 to each. Grill over charcoal until done to taste. Do not overcook! Baste shrimp generously with remaining marinade during grilling. Serve at once as an appetizer or entrée.

4 to 8 servings

Note: Combine 1 cup milk and 1 cup grated coconut in a saucepan. Bring quickly to boiling. Remove from the heat and set aside 30 minutes. Press out all the liquid and discard the coconut pulp.

Shrimp-Pineapple Kabobs

1 can (30 ounces) sliced pineapple
1 pound shrimp, fresh or frozen
¼ cup butter or margarine
1 tablespoon prepared mustard
  Juice of ½ lemon
  Salt and pepper to taste

1. Cut pineapple slices into fourths. Shell shrimp, leaving tail on. Cut down back of shrimp and remove vein.
2. To form each kabob, spear pineapple and shrimp onto skewer with 2 pieces of pineapple between shrimp. Arrange kabobs on a broiler rack.
3. Melt butter; stir in mustard, lemon juice, salt, and pepper. Brush sauce over kabobs. Grill 3 inches from coals about 5 minutes, brushing occasionally with remaining butter sauce.
4. To serve, slide kabobs from skewers onto plates, using fork.

About 4 servings

Seafood Kabobs

½ cup olive oil
3 tablespoons soy sauce
1 tablespoon Worcestershire sauce
2 tablespoons white wine vinegar
½ teaspoon grated lemon peel
2 tablespoons lemon juice
½ teaspoon freshly ground black pepper
2 teaspoons snipped parsley
1 lobster tail (8 ounces), cut in 6 pieces
6 scallops
6 shrimp, peeled, deveined, and rinsed
12 large mushroom caps
18 pieces sliced bacon (4 inch)
12 squares green pepper (1 inch)
6 cherry tomatoes

1. Combine first 8 ingredients in a screw-top jar and shake vigorously.
2. Pour the marinade over the seafood and mushroom caps and set aside for at least 2 hours. Drain, reserving marinade for brushing.
3. Wrap each piece of seafood in bacon. Thread pieces on 10-inch skewers as follows: green pepper, lobster, mushroom, scallop, mushroom, shrimp, and green pepper. Add a cherry tomato to each skewer during the last 5 minutes of grilling.
4. Grill 3 inches from coals 10 to 12 minutes, or until done, turning and brushing frequently with marinade.

6 kabobs

Perch Kabobs

2 pounds frozen ocean perch fillets
¼ cup salad oil
¼ cup lemon juice
2 tablespoons ketchup
1 teaspoon sugar
¾ teaspoon monosodium glutamate
½ teaspoon salt
¼ teaspoon paprika
¼ teaspoon dry mustard
1 teaspoon Worcestershire sauce
2 drops Tabasco
4 slices bacon, cut crosswise in fourths
2 large whole dill pickles, cut crosswise in eighths

1. While perch fillets are still frozen, cut them into 1½-inch chunks. Put into a large bowl or shallow dish and set aside.
2. Combine the salad oil and next 9 ingredients; blend well. Pour over fish chunks. Marinate 1½ hours at room temperature, turning chunks occasionally. Drain off and reserve marinade.
3. Thread onto each 5-inch skewer a fish chunk, a piece of bacon, and a piece of pickle. Repeat threading once and end with a fish chunk.
4. Place kabobs on a greased grill about 3 inches from hot coals. Turning frequently and brushing several times with reserved marinade, grill kabobs 12 to 15 minutes, or until fish flakes easily when tested with a fork. Serve with parsley-dipped lemon wedges, if desired.

About 8 kabobs

HOT OFF THE GRILL AND
DONE TO A TURN

Spit-Roasted Cornish Hens

3 Rock Cornish hens (1 pound each), at room temperature
Salt and pepper
½ cup olive oil, salad oil, or butter
¼ cup lemon juice
1 teaspoon salt
1 teaspoon marjoram
1 teaspoon thyme
½ teaspoon pepper
1 clove garlic, minced
2 tablespoons chopped chives

1. Season cavity of each hen with salt and pepper. Close neck and abdominal openings with skewers. Tie wings to bodies and tie legs together. Put a spit fork on rod. Dovetail hens and put second spit fork on rod. Insert spit forks in hens. Tighten screws with pliers. Attach spit with hens to rotisserie.
2. Combine the remaining ingredients and mix well. Start motor and brush hens with sauce. Roast over medium coals, about 6 inches from heat, until leg joints move easily and meat pulls away from leg bones, about 1 hour; brush frequently with sauce.
3. Split hens into halves with poultry shears or a sharp knife.

6 servings

Note: If using a gas-fired grill, sear hens for 2 minutes on high. Turn heat to medium and cook, brushing with sauce, until hens test done.

Glazed Chicken-on-a-Spit

2 broiler chickens (1½ to 2 pounds each)
2 teaspoons salt
Currant-Mustard Glaze

1. Remove spit from grill before building fire.
2. Rub cavities of birds with salt. Skewer neck skin to back; tuck wings against back. Carefully insert spit lengthwise through both birds. Be sure they are well balanced on the spit for even turning. Tie drumsticks to spit. Brush chickens with Currant-Mustard Glaze.
3. Attach spit; place drip pan in position. Start motor and grill about 1 hour, brushing frequently with glaze. Remove chickens from spit. Serve remaining glaze as a sauce, if desired.

4 servings

Currant-Mustard Glaze: Combine one (8-ounce) jar red currant jelly, ⅓ cup prepared mustard, and ½ teaspoon Tabasco in a small saucepan. Set over low heat until well blended and jelly is melted, stirring occasionally.

About 1 cup glaze

Turkey-on-a-Spit

1 turkey, 6 to 12 pounds (allow ¾ pound per serving)
1 to 2 teaspoons salt
Melted butter or margarine

1. Remove the spit from the grill before building the fire.
2. Rinse turkey well with cold water and pat dry. Rub cavity of turkey with salt. If desired, fill the body and neck cavities with stuffing. To close the body cavity, sew or skewer and lace with twine. Fasten neck skin to back with skewer. Loop twine around skewer and tie securely. Turn turkey breast-side up. Tuck wings in snugly to body; tie tightly with twine, using a figure eight pattern.
3. Insert spit rod with spit fork lengthwise through turkey, bringing rod out just above tail. Insert other spit fork in turkey. Test for balance. Tighten screws with pliers. Cross legs and tie firmly together. Tie tail and legs together tightly. Insert thermometer into center of inside thigh muscle or into center of breast. Thermometer must not touch bone or spit.
4. Attach spit and place drip pan in proper position; turn on motor. Brush turkey often during

roasting with drippings in pan and butter. Roast until done, allowing about 20 minutes per pound for unstuffed turkey and about 25 minutes per pound for stuffed turkey. Thermometer should register 180°F to 185°F when done.
5. When turkey is done, remove thermometer and take bird from spit; let stand 10 to 20 minutes before carving.

8 to 16 servings

Barbecued Turkey Roast

1 frozen boneless turkey roast (5 to 7 pounds), thawed
Salt and pepper
Melted butter or margarine
Savory Sweet-Tart Sauce (see recipe), or bottled barbecue sauce

1. If not preseasoned, rub surface of turkey roast with salt and pepper. Center roast on a motor-driven spit, following manufacturer's directions for roasts. Insert meat thermometer, being sure it does not touch spit. Brush roast with melted butter or margarine.
2. Roast turkey until done, 2½ to 3 hours (meat thermometer should register 170° to 175°F). During last 20 to 30 minutes, brush roast occasionally with Savory Sweet-Tart Sauce.
3. Remove roast from spit; let stand 15 minutes before slicing. Serve with additional sauce.

10 to 15 servings

Savory Sweet-Tart Sauce: Cook ¼ cup chopped onion in 1 tablespoon hot cooking or salad oil in a saucepan until soft. Add 1 cup bottled barbecue sauce, 1 cup unsweetened pineapple juice, 3 to 4 tablespoons dark corn syrup, ½ teaspoon grated lemon peel, 1 to 2 tablespoons lemon juice, 1 chicken bouillon cube, and a few grains ground ginger. Simmer until sauce is thickened, stirring occasionally.

About 1¾ cups sauce

Lamb Barbacoa

1 (6-pound) lamb leg or shoulder cushion roast, boneless, rolled and tied
1 cup water
1 cup port wine
½ cup olive oil
1 tablespoon salt
1 teaspoon freshly ground black pepper
⅛ teaspoon marjoram
⅛ teaspoon dry mustard
8 to 10 drops Tabasco
2 medium tomatoes, diced
1 medium green pepper, diced
1 medium onion, sliced
½ cup coarsely chopped parsley
3 cloves garlic, minced

1. Insert a skewer at intervals to make small holes all over lamb. Set lamb in a large shallow pan.
2. Combine and thoroughly blend the remaining ingredients and pour over the lamb. Cover and marinate about 24 hours in refrigerator; baste frequently, turning the lamb occasionally.
3. When ready to grill, remove the lamb from the marinade (reserve) and secure roast on spit, making sure it is evenly balanced. Insert meat thermometer so tip does not touch the spit or rest in fat; put drip pan in place and start motor.
4. Basting frequently with the liquid from the marinade, rotate on spit 2½ to 3 hours, or until meat thermometer registers 175°F for medium done or 180°F for well done.
5. Serve hot with the cold vegetable marinade as a relish.

8 to 12 servings

Pickle-Spiced Chicken-on-a-Spit

2 broiler-fryer chickens (2 pounds each)
1 cup sweet-pickle liquid
Salt and pepper

1. Pour pickle liquid over chickens. Cover and chill at least 2 hours; baste frequently and turn occasionally.
2. To grill, remove chickens from marinade, reserving marinade. Season chickens with salt and pepper and secure on rotisserie spit, making sure they are evenly balanced. Put drip pan in proper place in relation to coals and start rotisserie.
3. Basting frequently with marinade, rotate on spit about 1 hour, or until tender. Remove from spit and serve immediately.

4 servings

Hot Buttered Pineapple on the Spit

1 fresh pineapple
¼ cup butter or margarine
2 tablespoons brown sugar
⅛ teaspoon ground nutmeg
⅛ teaspoon ground cinnamon

1. Remove rind from pineapple by cutting from top to bottom with a sharp knife in strips; leaving leafy crown on. With a sharp-pointed knife, remove "eyes" of fruit by cutting spiral grooves. Place pineapple on spit rod, secure with spit forks, and test for balance. Wrap leafy crown with aluminum foil to protect from heat.
2. Melt butter and stir in brown sugar, nutmeg, and cinnamon; stir until blended.
3. Rotiss pineapple over medium heat, brushing occasionally with melted butter sauce until thoroughly heated, about 30 minutes. Slice to serve.

4 servings

Spit-Roasted Canadian Bacon

1 (1½-pound) piece smoked pork loin
    Canadian style bacon
⅔ cup bottled barbecue sauce
⅓ cup grape jelly

1. Secure meat on a spit and follow manufacturer's instructions for using rotisserie.
2. Beat barbecue sauce and grape jelly together.
3. Grill meat over medium coals, brushing with sauce every 15 minutes, for about 1½ hours, or until meat is heated throughout and reaches an internal temperature of 140°F; this internal temperature is for fully cooked pork.
4. Serve with the sauce, if desired.

About 6 servings

Note: A smoked pork shoulder roll may be prepared the same way; cook to 170°F.

Ham-on-a-Spit

Center a canned ham on a motor-driven spit, following grill manufacturer's directions. Roast until thoroughly heated and browned, brushing with a blend of apricot preserves and fruit juices.

HOT OFF THE GRILL AND
WRAPPED IN FOIL

Chuck Roast-Vegetable Supper Packet

Beef chuck blade roast, about 5 pounds
Garlic cloves, slivered
Dill weed
1½ tablespoons salt
1 cup ketchup
½ cup bottled steak sauce
½ cup cooking oil
¼ cup prepared horseradish
¼ cup wine vinegar
¼ cup dark corn syrup
2 teaspoons dry mustard
2 teaspoons salt
1 teaspoon pepper
1 teaspoon garlic powder
1 onion, chopped
1 carrot, pared and sliced
2 celery stalks, sliced
1 cup parsley, snipped
Onions, sliced
Carrots, pared and cut in half lengthwise
Potatoes, pared

1. Cut slits in surface of meat on both sides. Poke garlic slivers and a generous amount of dill weed into slits. Rub both sides of meat with the 1½ tablespoons salt.
2. Grill meat over hot coals 15 to 20 minutes on each side, or until brown.
3. Meanwhile, mix remaining ingredients, except vegetables, in a saucepan. Cook, stirring constantly, over low heat until mixture comes to boiling. Set aside.
4. Put the chopped onion, sliced carrot, celery, and parsley onto three thicknesses of heavy-duty aluminum foil in long lengths. Spoon some sauce over all. Transfer meat to the vegetable bed.
5. Surround and top meat with remaining vegetables (onions, carrots, and potatoes) and sauce.
6. Wrap tightly in foil, using a drugstore fold (avoid puncturing foil when handling the meat packet). Set on grill over low coals and turn every 30 minutes. Cook about 2 hours.

6 servings

Beef and Mushrooms Papillote

6 sheets (18×10 inch) heavy-duty
    aluminum foil
2½ pounds beef chuck pot roast, boneless,
    cut in cubes (about 1 inch)
2 teaspoons salt
1 teaspoon monosodium glutamate
½ teaspoon pepper
2 cloves garlic, minced
1 cup finely chopped parsley
2 tablespoons grated lemon peel
    Mushrooms, about 12 ounces, cleaned
    and quartered or sliced
2 white onions, cut in thin wedges

1. Toss the meat with the seasonings and then with remaining ingredients. Spoon mixture onto the sheets of foil. Tuck a small piece of bay leaf into each, if desired. Close packets with a drugstore fold and twist the ends tightly.
2. Set packets on grill over moderately hot coals. Cook slowly, turning packets over several times, about 1½ hours, or until meat is tender.

6 servings

Loaf o' Franks on a Grill

8 frankfurters
½ cup shredded sharp Cheddar cheese
3 tablespoons finely chopped mushrooms
3 tablespoons finely chopped pitted green
    olives
2 tablespoons finely chopped onion
2 tablespoons ketchup
2 cloves garlic, minced
½ teaspoon Worcestershire sauce
½ teaspoon salt
¾ cup butter or margarine
¾ teaspoon dry mustard
1 loaf French bread
2 teaspoons sesame seed

1. Make a slit almost through each frankfurter. Mix cheese and the next 7 ingredients. Fill each frankfurter; set aside.
2. Cream butter and mustard together; set aside.
3. Use an apple corer to diagonally cut holes about 1½ inches in diameter and 1 inch apart into sides and through the loaf of bread.
4. Spread cavities with about a third of the mustard butter. Insert filled frankfurters, allowing ends to extend equally from each side. Spread about a quarter of remaining mustard butter on the bottom of loaf and remainder on top. Top with sesame seed.
5. Wrap loaf in heavy-duty aluminum foil and seal tightly, using drugstore fold. Place loaf to one side of grill over warm, not hot, coals. Grill 30 to 40 minutes, or until frankfurters are heated and bread is crisp; turn several times.
6. To serve, unwrap and slice loaf diagonally between frankfurters.

8 servings

Chicken in Pineapple Barbecue Sauce

**Chicken breasts and legs, rinsed, dried,
    and seasoned**
1 cup bottled barbecue sauce
1 can (8¼ ounces) crushed pineapple
1 can (11 ounces) mandarin oranges, drained

1. Brown chicken on both sides over hot coals on a grill. For each serving, transfer 1 chicken breast and 1 leg to a length of heavy-duty aluminum foil. Turn up edges of foil.
2. Blend barbecue sauce, crushed pineapple, and oranges in a saucepan. Heat thoroughly, about 10 minutes. Spoon desired amount over chicken pieces on the foil.
3. Bring two opposite edges of foil together and wrap securely, using a drugstore fold and turning up ends to seal. Cook over medium coals about 25 minutes, turning packets once or twice.
4. If desired, serve with iced relishes and bowls of potato and corn chips.

4 to 6 servings

Barbecued Turkey Drumsticks

  1 can (8 ounces) tomato sauce with tomato
    bits
  ¼ cup molasses
  ¼ cup lemon juice
  1 tablespoon Worcestershire sauce
  ¼ teaspoon Tabasco
  1 tablespoon chopped chives
  1 teaspoon marjoram leaves
  ¼ teaspoon salt
  6 turkey drumsticks (about 1 pound each)
    Salt and pepper
    Butter

1. For sauce, combine tomato sauce, molasses, lemon juice, Worcestershire sauce, Tabasco, chives, marjoram, and salt. Refrigerate overnight to blend flavors.
2. Put each turkey leg on a piece of heavy-duty aluminum foil. Sprinkle with salt and pepper and dot with butter. Wrap securely, using a drugstore fold and sealing ends.
3. Set packages on grill 3 to 6 inches from heat. Grill about 2 hours, or until fork-tender, turning occasionally.
4. Remove foil and brush drumsticks with sauce. Grill about 20 minutes, turning frequently and brushing with sauce.

6 servings

Note: Sauce may be used as a brushing sauce for hamburgers or frankfurters during grilling.

Vegetable-Stuffed Chicken

  6 whole broiler-fryer chicken breasts, rinsed
    and boned
    Vegetable Stuffing (see recipe)
    Butter or margarine
  1 teaspoon salt
  ¼ teaspoon pepper
  ½ teaspoon paprika

1. Place each boned breast, skin side down, onto a square of heavy-duty aluminum foil. Spoon about 2½ tablespoons stuffing onto center of each breast; overlap sides of chicken, covering stuffing. Turn overlapped side down on the foil.
2. Brush chicken with butter and sprinkle with salt, pepper, and paprika. For each packet, bring two opposite edges of foil together over chicken and wrap securely, using a drugstore fold and turning up ends to seal.
3. Set packets on a hot grill; cook 35 to 45 minutes, or until chicken is tender, turning packets over twice during cooking.
4. Transfer chicken from foil to individual plates.

6 servings

Vegetable Stuffing

  ¼ cup butter or margarine
  ½ cup diced celery
  ¼ cup diced carrot
  ¼ cup diced green pepper
  4 green onions, thinly sliced
  ½ teaspoon salt
  ¼ teaspoon monosodium glutamate
  3 tablespoons snipped parsley
  ½ teaspoon chervil leaves, crushed
  ¼ teaspoon marjoram leaves, crushed

1. Heat butter or margarine in a small skillet. Add celery, carrot, green pepper, and green onion. Sprinkle with the salt and monosodium glutamate. Cook over low heat 2 to 3 minutes, stirring occasionally.
2. Remove from heat and mix in the parsley and dried herbs.

About 1 cup stuffing

Frank-Vegetable Medley

    18-inch heavy-duty aluminum foil, 4 long
      lengths
  2 tablespoons wine vinegar
  1 clove garlic, minced
  2 teaspoons salt
  ½ teaspoon chili powder
  ¼ teaspoon oregano leaves, crushed
  ¼ teaspoon basil leaves, crushed
  6 tablespoons olive, or other salad, oil
  2 large zucchini, sliced
  2 large ripe tomatoes, cut in wedges
  1 small green pepper, cut in strips
  6 green onions with tops, sliced
  ¼ cup snipped parsley
  8 frankfurters
    Bottled barbecue sauce

1. Pour wine vinegar into a bottle or jar having a tight-fitting cover. Add garlic; then salt, chili powder, oregano, and basil. Cover and shake well. Add oil; shake until blended. Set aside.

2. Bring edges of each foil piece up slightly. Divide zucchini, tomato, green pepper, green onion, and parsley evenly among the packets. Vigorously shake mixture in bottle and spoon about 2 tablespoons evenly over vegetables in each packet.

3. Slit franks almost through lengthwise, spread cut surfaces generously with barbecue sauce, and gently press together. Put 2 franks into each packet.

4. For each packet, bring two opposite edges of foil together over mixture and wrap securely, using a drugstore fold; turn up ends and fold to seal.

5. Set packets on a hot grill; cook 20 to 25 minutes, turning packets over once. Open packets and gently mix vegetables and franks with their juices before serving. If desired, serve with crusty bread which has been wrapped in foil and heated on the grill.

4 servings

Fish Fiesta Packets

 Olive Sauce (see recipe)
 Salmon or halibut steaks, cut ½ to ¾ inch
  thick (allow 5 ounces per serving)
 6 slices eggplant, cut ¼ inch thick
 6 slices lemon
 6 slices onion
 6 slices tomato

1. Spoon 1 tablespoon Olive Sauce onto center of each of 6 (12-inch) squares of heavy-duty aluminum foil; bring edges of foil up slightly.

2. Place salmon or halibut steaks on the sauce. Spoon 2 tablespoons of the Olive Sauce over each steak. Add one slice of eggplant, lemon, onion, and tomato to each steak, spooning some of the remaining sauce over each layer.

3. Wrap packets securely. Grill 3 inches from coals 25 to 30 minutes.

6 packets

Olive Sauce: In a screw-top jar, combine ¾ cup olive oil, ¼ cup lemon juice, 2 tablespoons Worcestershire sauce, 1½ teaspoons salt, ¼ teaspoon black pepper, 1 teaspoon savory, and 1 cup chopped pimento-stuffed olives. Shake vigorously before using.

About 2 cups sauce

Fish Dinner Deluxe in Foil

 ½ cup butter or margarine
 ½ cup chopped celery
 ½ cup chopped onion
 ½ pound fresh mushrooms, sliced
 ½ teaspoon salt
 ¼ teaspoon pepper
 2 teaspoons Worcestershire sauce
 2 cups coarsely crumbled saltines
 ¼ cup finely snipped parsley
 6 fish fillets (sole or flounder)
 6 tomatoes
 6 ears sweet corn, husked and brushed with
  melted butter
 Salt

1. Heat the butter or margarine in a skillet. Add celery, onion, and mushrooms; cook 5 minutes or until mushrooms are lightly browned, stirring occasionally.

2. Mix in the salt, pepper, and Worcestershire sauce, then the crumbled saltines and parsley; blend thoroughly.

3. Form a ring with each fish fillet, overlapping ends and fastening with wooden picks. Place each rolled fillet on an 18-inch square of heavy-duty aluminum foil.

4. Fill each fillet with stuffing, reserving 6 tablespoons. Cut out stem end from each tomato and fill with 1 tablespoon of the stuffing. Add a tomato and an ear of corn to each packet. Sprinkle each ear of corn lightly with salt.

5. Wrap packets securely, using drugstore wrap. Place on grill 3 inches from coals and cook 10 minutes. Turn packet and cook 10 minutes longer, or until fish and vegetables are done.

6 packets

Savory Outdoor Baked Fish

Scale and clean fish, leaving whole. Place fish on individual sheets of heavy-duty aluminum foil and brush with melted butter or oil. Sprinkle with salt and pepper and drizzle with lemon juice. Top each fish with a teaspoonful of chopped tomato or pimento and garnish with lemon slices. Bring foil up over fish and seal with a double fold. Seal ends. Place on grill over a medium-hot fire and cook 10 minutes on a side for a small 1- to 1½-pound fish, 15 minutes on a side for 2- to 3-pound fish, and about 20 minutes on a side for 4- to 5-pound fish. Open foil; if fish flakes easily when tested with a fork, it is done. Serve with juices from bottom of package.

Back-Yard Clambake

18-inch heavy-duty aluminum foil, 28-inch length
Cheesecloth
Seaweed or rockweed (available at fish market), thoroughly washed
1 dozen unopened steamer clams, well scrubbed and rinsed
Half of a 2½-pound broiler-fryer chicken (split lengthwise), rinsed
1 lobster (1 to 1¼ pounds), well rinsed
1 ready-to-cook ear of corn (fresh or frozen)
1 baking potato, scrubbed, rinsed, and cut lengthwise in quarters

1. For each packet, line the length of foil with a piece of cheesecloth several inches longer than foil.
2. Form three layers on the piece of cheesecloth using seaweed, clams, chicken, and lobster in that order. Tuck in the corn ear (halves, if long) and potato quarters. Sprinkle lightly with salt and grind pepper over all . Bring the cheesecloth up to cover the food. Bring two opposite edges of foil together over mixture and wrap securely, using a drugstore fold; turn up ends and fold to seal.
3. Set packet on a hot grill and cook 1 hour, or until chicken is tender. (Cover grill with hood if necessary during cooking.)
4. Carefully pour the broth from packet into a cup for dunking the clams or for drinking. Accompany with melted butter or margarine. Serve with crusty bread, which has been wrapped in foil and heated on grill; slice before serving.

1 serving

Note: If substituting South African rock lobster tails for the lobster, put 2 small tails, still frozen, on seaweed with the clams, then chicken, corn, and quartered potato. If clams are not used, pour ¼ cup canned clam juice cocktail over all along with the seasonings.

Grill-Baked Eggs au Gratin

8 slices Canadian-style bacon (about 8 ounces)
4 English muffins, split
Melted butter or margarine
8 eggs
Salt and pepper
¼ cup butter or margarine
¼ cup water
1 jar (5 ounces) pasteurized process sharp Cheddar cheese spread
½ teaspoon dry mustard
2 egg yolks, beaten

1. Grill Canadian bacon slices over prepared coals until brown. Wrap in aluminum foil and keep warm at edge of grill.
2. Toast English muffins on grill; keep warm on edge of grill.
3. Cut eight 6-inch squares of heavy-duty aluminum foil. Make foil cups by molding each square around bottom of a 1-pound can. Brush each cup with a little melted butter. Break each egg into a custard cup and slip into foil cup. Place eggs in foil cups on grill. Cook until eggs are set. Season with salt and pepper.
4. While eggs are cooking, make cheese sauce. In a small saucepan, heat butter, water, cheese spread, and mustard on grill until melted and

smooth. Add a small amount of hot mixture to egg yolks and turn into pan. Cook and stir until thickened and smooth.

5. To serve, place Canadian bacon slices on toasted English muffins. Run a spatula around eggs, remove from foil, and place on Canadian bacon. Spoon cheese sauce over each serving.

4 servings

Shrimp-Green Pepper Packets

1 pound shrimp, peeled, deveined, and rinsed
½ cup bottled barbecue sauce
1 large green pepper, cut in long ¼-inch strips
1 clove garlic, crushed in a garlic press or minced
1 teaspoon grated onion
½ cup butter or margarine
1 teaspoon salt
⅛ teaspoon pepper
½ teaspoon ground ginger
½ teaspoon dry mustard
¼ cup lime juice
1 tablespoon honey
8 drops Tabasco

1. Combine shrimp and barbecue sauce; turn shrimp to coat well with sauce. Set aside.
2. Divide green pepper equally on center of 4 large pieces of heavy-duty aluminum foil. Bring edges of foil up slightly to hold sauce.
3. Stir garlic and onion into hot butter in a skillet; cook 2 minutes. Remove from heat. Blend salt, pepper, ginger, and dry mustard; add to garlic mixture with the remaining ingredients. Pour the seasoned butter over green pepper.
4. Divide the shrimp and sauce equally among

the 4 packets. Bring edges of foil up over mixture and seal tightly, using drugstore wrap.
5. Place on grill 3 to 4 inches from coals and cook about 20 minutes; turn packets over once to cook shrimp evenly.

4 packets

Shrimp-Bologna Packets

18-inch heavy-duty aluminum foil, 4 long lengths
2 pounds fresh shrimp, peeled, deveined, and rinsed
1 pound bologna (casing removed), cut in thick 3-inch strips
2 large green peppers, cut in long ¼-inch strips
Celery, cut diagonally in 1-inch lengths
16 tablespoons butter or margarine
2 cups bottled barbecue sauce with onion

1. Bring edges of each length of foil up slightly. Divide shrimp, bologna, green pepper, and celery equally among the packets. Put 4 tablespoons butter or margarine into each packet. Pour one-half cup sauce into each packet.
2. For each packet, bring two opposite edges of foil together over mixture and wrap tightly, using a drugstore fold; turn up ends and fold to seal.
3. Set packets over hot coals on grill. Cook 15 to 20 minutes, or until shrimp are tender; turn packets over once during cooking. Open packets and gently mix shrimp with sauce before serving.

4 servings

Mixed Bean Packet

1 package (9 ounces) frozen cut green beans
1 package (9 ounces) frozen cut wax beans
1 package (10 ounces) frozen lima beans
1 teaspoon salt
⅛ teaspoon pepper
¼ teaspoon ground mace
¼ cup chopped onion
¼ cup butter or margarine, cut in pieces

1. Partially thaw frozen vegetables; toss lightly with remaining ingredients. Put in center of a large square of heavy-duty aluminum foil; wrap and seal.
2. Cook on grill until tender, about 15 minutes.

About 8 servings

Zucchini Packet

6 small zucchini, cut crosswise in ¼-inch slices
1 medium onion, halved and thinly sliced
½ teaspoon salt
¼ teaspoon pepper
1 tablespoon brown sugar
1 beef bouillon cube, crushed
¼ teaspoon crushed fennel seed
3 tablespoons butter or margarine, cut in pieces

1. Put zucchini and onion onto center of a large square of heavy-duty aluminum foil. Sprinkle with salt, pepper, brown sugar, bouillon cube, and fennel seed, then dot with butter. Wrap and seal.
2. Cook on grill 20 minutes, or until tender.

4 to 6 servings

Wax Bean Packet

1 package (9 ounces) frozen wax beans, partially thawed
½ medium green pepper, cut in strips
¼ cup sliced green onion (with tops)
¼ pound fresh mushrooms, sliced
½ teaspoon salt
⅛ teaspoon freshly ground black pepper
¼ teaspoon paprika
½ clove garlic, minced
3 tablespoons butter or margarine, cut in pieces

1. Put the beans, green pepper, onion, and mushrooms in center of a large square of heavy-duty aluminum foil. Sprinkle with salt, pepper, and paprika. Mix in garlic. Top with butter. Wrap and seal.
2. Cook on grill until tender, about 15 minutes.

About 4 servings

Grilled Tomato Halves

Cut 4 medium to large tomatoes into halves horizontally. Place each tomato half, cut side up, in center of a 6-inch square of aluminum foil. Combine 2 teaspoons sweet basil and 2 teaspoons seasoned salt. Sprinkle mixture evenly over tomatoes. Mix ½ cup chopped green pepper, ½ cup shredded Parmesan cheese, and 2 cloves garlic, minced. Top each tomato half with 2 tablespoons of the mixture. Bring corners of foil up over each tomato half and seal lightly. Place on grill over hot coals and cook about 10 minutes, or until cheese is melted.

8 tomato halves

Zucchini-Tomato Packet

6 small zucchini, cut crosswise in ¼-inch slices
1 medium onion, halved and thinly sliced
2 tomatoes, cut in small pieces
¼ cup shredded Cheddar cheese
1 teaspoon salt
Few grains black pepper
3 tablespoons butter or margarine, cut in pieces
2 tablespoons soy sauce

1. Mix all ingredients and put onto center of a large square of heavy-duty aluminum foil; wrap and seal.
2. Cook on grill 20 minutes, or until tender.

4 to 6 servings

Pilaf in a Pouch

6 cups cooked rice
1 package (10 ounces) frozen peas, partially thawed
1 can (5 ounces) water chestnuts, drained and sliced
½ cup chopped green onion (with tops)
2 medium tomatoes, cut in thin wedges
¾ cup butter or margarine
1½ teaspoons seasoned salt
Freshly ground black pepper
1½ teaspoons basil, crushed

1. Make 8 pouches from 18×12-inch pieces of heavy-duty aluminum foil by pressing each sheet of foil into a small bowl to form pouch; remove from bowl.
2. Divide all ingredients equally into the 8 pouches. Seal each pouch securely.
3. Place pouches on grill over hot coals for 15 minutes, or until mixture is thoroughly heated.
4. Open foil and fluff mixture with a fork before serving.

8 servings

Note: Pouches may be filled several hours in advance of grilling.

Mace-Flavored Green Beans in Packet

    2 packages (9 ounces each) frozen cut green
        beans, partially thawed
    ½ pound sliced fresh mushrooms
    ¼ cup chopped onion
    1 teaspoon salt
    ⅛ teaspoon pepper
    ¼ teaspoon ground mace
    ¼ cup butter or margarine

1. Put beans, mushrooms, and onion onto center of a large square of heavy-duty aluminum foil. Break beans apart, if necessary.
2. Sprinkle a mixture of seasonings over vegetables and dot with butter. Bring foil up over contents and seal tightly, using drugstore wrap.
3. Place packet on grill about 5 inches from coals and cook about 35 minutes, or until beans are just tender; turn packet over once during the cooking period.
4. If desired, top with or blend in chopped salted almonds before serving.

About 8 servings

Cheese-Topped Tomatoes in Packets

    Large ripe tomatoes, cut crosswise into halves
    Seasoned salt
    Chopped chives
    Creamy Roquefort or blue cheese salad
        dressing

1. Place each tomato half in the center of a 6-inch square of heavy-duty aluminum foil. Sprinkle cut surfaces of tomatoes with salt and chives. Top with dressing. Bring corners of foil up over tomatoes.
2. Cook on grill 3 to 5 minutes.

1 tomato half per serving

Whole Tomatoes in Foil

    6 tomatoes
    1½ teaspoons salt
    ¾ teaspoon pepper
    1½ teaspoons basil
    2 tablespoons butter or margarine
    1 clove garlic, crushed in a garlic press or
        minced

1. Cut off stem ends of tomatoes. Hold each tomato upside down and gently squeeze out juice and seeds.
2. Place tomatoes, right side up, on pieces of heavy-duty aluminum foil. Sprinkle with salt, pepper, and basil. Add butter and garlic. Seal packets securely.
3. Set packets on grill over hot coals and cook about 20 minutes, or until tomatoes are tender.

6 servings

Tomatoes in Foil

    4 large tomatoes
    Salt
    Freshly ground black pepper
    8 teaspoons butter or margarine
    ¼ cup chopped parsley
    ⅓ cup chopped green onion with tops
    1 teaspoon basil, crushed
    1 teaspoon tarragon, crushed
    1 clove garlic, crushed

1. Halve tomatoes crosswise. Sprinkle cut surfaces generously with salt and pepper; top each half with 1 teaspoon butter.
2. Mix remaining ingredients and mound equally on each tomato half. Set 4 tomato halves on each of 2 large pieces of heavy-duty aluminum foil; wrap and seal tightly. Grill 3 inches from coals about 10 minutes, or until just tender (not mushy).

8 servings

Carrot-Celery-Green Pepper Packet

> 2 cups raw carrot slices (¼ inch)
> 2 cups diagonally cut celery slices (½ inch)
> 2 cups green pepper pieces (½ inch)
> ¼ cup cooking or salad oil
> 2 teaspoons salt
> ⅛ teaspoon black pepper
> 1 teaspoon dill weed

1. Measure all ingredients onto a large square of heavy-duty aluminum foil; wrap and seal.
2. Cook on grill 35 minutes.

8 servings

Fennel-Flavored Vegetable Packet

> 2 tomatoes, cut in wedges
> 1 cup finger-size pieces eggplant
> 1 medium onion, sliced
> 2 zucchini, sliced
> 1 tablespoon brown sugar
> 1 beef bouillon cube, crushed
> ½ teaspoon salt
> ⅛ teaspoon pepper
> ¼ teaspoon crushed fennel seed
> 3 tablespoons butter, cut in pieces

1. Toss all ingredients lightly in a bowl. Put onto center of a large square of heavy-duty aluminum foil. Seal packet securely, using drugstore wrap.
2. Place on grill 5 inches from coals and cook about 30 minutes, turning packet over once.

About 4 servings

Pineapple-Rice and Ham Packets

> 3 cups freshly cooked rice
> 1 can (20 ounces) crushed pineapple, drained
> ¼ cup firmly packed brown sugar
> ¼ cup butter or margarine
> ¼ cup diced green pepper
> 1 tablespoon soy sauce
> 1 teaspoon prepared mustard
> 8 slices cooked ham (8 ounces)

1. Combine rice with pineapple, brown sugar, butter, green pepper, soy sauce, and mustard.

2. Put a ham slice on each of 8 squares of heavy-duty aluminum foil. Spoon rice mixture onto ham. Wrap securely, using drugstore fold and sealing ends.
3. Set packets on grill over hot coals until heated, about 15 minutes.

8 servings

Green Bean-Squash Medley

> 1 package (10 ounces) frozen cut green beans, partially thawed and broken apart
> 1 pound yellow summer squash, sliced and cut in small wedges
> 2 medium onions, thinly sliced
> 1 pimento, cut in strips
> 3 tablespoons butter
> 2 teaspoons seasoned salt
> ¼ teaspoon freshly ground black pepper

1. Mix first 4 ingredients on a large double piece of heavy-duty aluminum foil. Dot with the butter and sprinkle with the salt and pepper. Using a drugstore wrap, seal packet tightly.
2. Grill about 3 inches from source of heat, turning occasionally, 40 to 50 minutes, or until vegetables are tender.

6 to 8 servings

Herbed Vegetable Medley

> 4 medium zucchini, cut crosswise into ½-inch slices
> 1 or 2 large tomatoes, cut in pieces
> 1 medium onion, thinly sliced
> ½ teaspoon basil
> ¼ teaspoon thyme
> ¼ teaspoon marjoram
> ½ teaspoon salt
> Few grains freshly ground black pepper
> ¼ cup highly seasoned French dressing (preferably with wine vinegar)

1. Put the zucchini, tomatoes, onion, and remaining ingredients in the center of a large square of heavy-duty aluminum foil. Bring corners of foil up over vegetables; seal tightly.
2. Cook on grill about 20 minutes, or until zucchini is tender but not mushy. If desired, sprinkle with seasoned salt before serving.

6 to 8 servings

Vegetable Medley in Foil

3 medium zucchini, cut in ½-inch slices
7 large mushrooms, sliced lengthwise
 through caps and stems
1 large tomato, cut in pieces
3 medium onions, thinly sliced
8 large pimento-stuffed green olives, sliced
3 tablespoons olive oil
1 clove garlic, crushed
1 teaspoon parsley flakes
½ teaspoon sweet basil
1 teaspoon salt
 Freshly ground black pepper

1. Toss the vegetables and olives together in the center of a large square of heavy-duty aluminum foil; gently mix in remaining ingredients. Bring edges of foil up over mixture and seal tightly to avoid leakage when packet is turned.
2. Place on grill about 3 inches from coals and cook 15 to 20 minutes, or until zucchini is tender. Turn packet over occasionally to cook vegetables evenly.

4 to 6 servings

Peas in Foil Packet

2 packages (10 ounces each) frozen green
 peas, slightly thawed
1 cup sliced green onion (with tops)
½ pound fresh mushrooms, sliced lengthwise
2 teaspoons celery seed
1 teaspoon sugar
1 teaspoon salt
¼ teaspoon freshly ground black pepper
6 tablespoons butter or margarine

1. Put peas, onion, and mushrooms onto center of a large square of heavy-duty aluminum foil.

2. Mix celery seed, sugar, salt, and pepper and sprinkle over peas. Dot with butter. Bring corners of foil up over peas and seal tightly.
3. Place packet on grill about 5 inches from coals and cook about 35 minutes, or until peas are just tender; turn packet over once during cooking.

About 10 servings

Dilled Potatoes in Packets

6 medium potatoes, pared
 Salt
½ cup butter or margarine, softened
2 tablespoons snipped parsley
1 tablespoon dill weed

1. Cut each potato crosswise into 1-inch slices and place on an individual square of heavy-duty aluminum foil. Sprinkle slices generously with salt and spread with butter. Sprinkle evenly with snipped parsley and dill weed.
2. Put slices together to reassemble each potato; wrap in foil, sealing tightly.
3. Place on grill 3 inches from coals and cook about 35 minutes, or until potatoes are tender. Turn packets occasionally to cook evenly.

6 servings

Ratatouille in Packets

6 eggplant slices
6 onion slices
6 tomato slices
12 zucchini slices
 Olive oil
1 clove garlic, crushed in a garlic press or
 minced
2 teaspoons salt
½ teaspoon pepper
2 teaspoons basil

1. On 6 pieces of heavy-duty aluminum foil, make stacks of vegetables, brushing layers with olive oil and seasoning with garlic, salt, pepper, and basil. Pour 1 teaspoon olive oil on each stack. Seal packets securely, using drugstore wrap.
2. Set packets on grill over hot coals and cook about 30 minutes, turning over several times.

6 servings

Corn in Foil

Remove husks, silk, and blemishes from ears of corn. Place each ear on a piece of heavy-duty aluminum foil. Brush generously with Golden Glow Butter. Wrap foil around ears, sealing edges with double folds. Cook on grill about 15 minutes, turning frequently. Partially unwrap and serve corn in foil with a bowl of Golden Glow Butter and a shaker of salt.

Corn on the Grill

Loosen husks only enough to remove silks and blemishes from ears of corn. Dip ears in water. Shake well. Rewrap husks around corn. Plunge into water again and let stand until husks are soaked, about 1 hour. Place ears over coals and roast, turning frequently, until tender, about 15 minutes. Immediately husk the corn, brush with Golden Glow Butter or Perky Butter Sauce, and sprinkle with salt.

Golden Glow Butter: Heat together ½ cup butter or margarine, 2 tablespoons sieved pimento, ½ teaspoon onion juice, ¼ teaspoon paprika, ⅛ teaspoon salt, and a few grains black pepper.

Perky Butter Sauce: Heat together ½ cup butter or margarine, ½ teaspoon dry Italian salad dressing mix, ½ teaspoon paprika, and ¼ teaspoon chili powder. Serve hot.

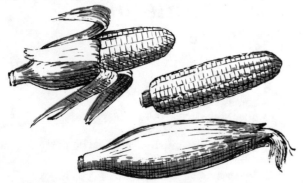

Roasted Potatoes in Foil

Scrub, dry, and rub potatoes with fat. Wrap in aluminum foil, sealing edges with double folds. Place on grill about 1 hour, or until potatoes are soft when pressed with glove-protected fingers. Turn several times. Loosen foil, cut a cross in top each potato, and pinch open. Spoon Herb Butter into each potato. Top with grated cheese. Rewrap; grill to melt cheese.

Herb Butter: Blend ½ cup softened butter with 2 teaspoons minced parsley, 1 teaspoon crushed sweet basil, and 1 teaspoon crushed tarragon.

Potatoes Baked in Coals

Wash and scrub large baking potatoes and bury in the coals for 45 minutes to 1 hour. Potatoes are done when they can be easily pierced with a fork.

Garlic Bread

> 1 loaf French bread
> 1 clove garlic
> ¼ teaspoon salt
> ½ cup softened butter or margarine

1. Make diagonal cuts from ½ to ¾ inch apart almost through bread.
2. Crush garlic with salt to form a smooth paste. Blend with butter. Spread butter between slices and on top of bread. Place loaf on a piece of aluminum foil large enough to cover bread completely. Wrap loaf loosely, closing ends with a double fold.
3. Set on grill about 10 minutes, or until heated entirely through; turn frequently for even heating. Serve piping hot.

1 loaf garlic bread

Cheesy English Muffin Splits

> ¼ cup butter or margarine
> 2 tablespoons snipped chives
> ¼ teaspoon garlic salt
> ¼ teaspoon oregano
> 1 teaspoon Worcestershire sauce
> 2 drops Tabasco
> 15 ounces (3 jars) pasteurized process cheese spread
> 14 large English muffin halves, grilled and buttered

1. Cream the butter with chives, garlic salt, oregano, Worcestershire sauce, and Tabasco; beat in the cheese. Spread on the grilled English muffins.
2. Heat on aluminum foil on grill.

14 muffin halves

Kettle Patio Potatoes

Scrub long white baking potatoes. Cut each lengthwise into 4 or 5 slices. Place sliced potatoes on double-thick pieces of heavy-duty aluminum foil. Pour 1 tablespoon cream over each, dot with 1½ teaspoons butter, and sprinkle with ¼ teaspoon salt and few grains pepper. Seal securely, using drugstore fold and turning up ends. Set on grill to cook 45 to 60 minutes.

French Fries in a Poke

Put partially thawed frozen French fried potatoes onto a large square of heavy-duty aluminum foil. Sprinkle with salt and pepper. Gather foil up around potatoes, partially closing at top. Set on the grill over hot coals and heat, shaking the package occasionally, 15 minutes, or until potatoes are hot to the touch.

Baked Sweet Potatoes in Foil

4 sweet potatoes
Vegetable shortening
4 teaspoons brown sugar
4 teaspoons butter or margarine

1. Wash, scrub, and dry sweet potatoes. Rub shortening over entire surface of potatoes and wrap each loosely in aluminum foil. Seal open ends with a double fold.
2. Place on grill and bake about 45 minutes, or until tender. Turn several times for even baking.
3. Loosen foil. Make a slit in top of each. Put brown sugar and butter on top.

4 servings

Barbecue Pit Potatoes

Pare 4 large baking potatoes and cut each lengthwise into 6 or 8 chunks. Place on a large square of heavy-duty aluminum foil. Brush potatoes with melted butter and sprinkle with salt and black pepper. Bring corners of foil together and gently squeeze edges to seal; place on grill. Shift package occasionally on grill to insure even cooking. Cook about 55 minutes, or until potatoes are tender; open foil the last few minutes to allow steam to escape. Sprinkle with seasoned salt and serve.

8 servings

Dilled Onion Packet

1 large Bermuda onion
1 teaspoon butter or margarine
½ teaspoon dill weed
Seasoned salt

1. Peel and partially core the onion (allow 1 for each serving). Put the butter and dill weed into cavity; sprinkle generously with the seasoned salt. Wrap in a square of heavy-duty aluminum foil.
2. Cook on grill 1 to 1½ hours. Serve topped with dairy sour cream.

1 serving

Grilled Whole Onions

Leave dry outer skins on Spanish or Bermuda onions. Wet thoroughly and place on grill about 50 minutes, or until onions are black outside and soft and creamy inside. Roll occasionally to cook evenly.

Baked Apples in Foil

6 large baking apples
¼ cup raisins
¼ cup chopped walnuts
1 tablespoon grated orange peel
¼ cup honey
¼ cup orange juice

1. Core apples and pare a 1-inch strip around top of each. Fill cavities with raisins and nuts.
2. Place apples on large pieces of heavy-duty aluminum foil. Mix orange peel with honey and spoon over filled apples. Pour orange juice over tops and wrap apples securely, using drugstore fold and sealing ends.
3. Set on grill about 3 inches from hot coals and cook about 1 hour, or until tender.
4. Serve hot or cool with cream, if desired.

6 servings

GUIDE FOR THE

How to Grill

Marinades and Sauces

RIBS (pork)

Spareribs and back ribs—Marinate, if desired. Place on a rack in a large shallow pan. Cover with foil; partially cook in a 350°F oven 30 minutes. (If done in advance and refrigerated, return to room temperature.) To grill, place 6 to 8 inches from coals and brush with marinade or sauce. Grill 40 to 50 minutes, or until meat is done, turning and brushing frequently. (To grill ribs without precooking: grill over a drip pan about 2 hours, turning occasionally. Brush frequently with sauce last 40 minutes.)

Pineapple marinade—Blend 1 cup honey, 1 cup unsweetened pineapple juice, 2 cups (2 8¼-oz. cans) crushed pineapple, ⅔ cup red wine vinegar, 2 tablespoons soy sauce, 6 large cloves garlic, crushed, 2 tablespoons ground ginger, 1 tablespoon ground coriander, 1 teaspoon salt, and ½ cup chopped onion in a large skillet. Cook over medium heat, stirring occasionally, about 40 minutes, or until thickened. Reserve 1 cup to heat and serve with ribs. Marinate ribs (4 pounds) 24 hours.

Single ribs for appetizers—Have meat dealer saw spareribs (unnecessary for back ribs) across rib bones, if desired. Precook as directed above. Cut into individual ribs. Arrange in a hinged basket broiler and brush with marinade or sauce. Grill 6 inches from coals 40 to 50 minutes, turning and brushing frequently.

Piquant tomato sauce—Mix and simmer 10 minutes 1 cup ketchup, ¼ cup lemon juice, 1 tablespoon soy sauce, 2 tablespoons brown sugar, 1 tablespoon prepared horseradish mustard, 1 tablespoon grated onion, 1½ teaspoons salt, ½ teaspoon black pepper, ¼ teaspoon oregano, ¼ teaspoon Tabasco, and 1 split clove garlic.

STEAKS (beef)

Porterhouse, sirloin, T-bone, or rib (1½ inches thick)—Marinate, if desired. Grill 3 inches from coals (brushing frequently with marinade, if used). When well browned, turn and season or continue brushing. Total grilling time: 12 minutes for rare. For medium or well done, increase distance from coals and grilling time.

Claret marinade—Mix ¾ cup olive oil, ¾ cup claret, 3 large cloves garlic, crushed, 4 drops Tabasco, ½ teaspoon dry mustard, 1 teaspoon ground nutmeg, and ¼ cup finely chopped pimento-stuffed olives. Marinate steaks or beef cubes for kabobs 6 hours or overnight, turning occasionally; reserve marinade for brushing.

CHOPS (lamb)

Grill chops (1½ inches thick) 4 inches from coals (brushing often with sauce, if used). When well browned, turn; season or continue brushing. Total grilling time: 16 minutes for medium done.

Mint sauce—Stir together ½ cup water, ¼ cup lemon juice, 12 fresh mint leaves, crushed, 2 split cloves garlic, 2 tablespoons chopped onion, and 1 teaspoon rosemary. Let stand overnight.

KABOBS (lamb or beef)

Thread marinated meat cubes (1 to 1½ inches) onto skewers. Place close together for rare meat or separate for well done. Grill 3 inches from coals 15 to 20 minutes or until tender and browned, turning and brushing frequently with marinade.

Caper marinade for lamb—Mix ½ cup cider vinegar, ½ cup sweet pickle liquid, ⅓ cup olive oil, 1 tablespoon dry mustard, 1 teaspoon salt, ½ teaspoon pepper, and 2 tablespoons capers. Marinate lamb 6 hours. **Claret marinade for beef**, see steaks.

OUTDOOR CHEF

How to Grill

Grill burgers (1 inch thick) in a hinged basket broiler or on a greased grill 4 to 5 inches from coals (brushing frequently with sauce, if used). When browned, turn and season or continue brushing. Total grilling time: 10 minutes for medium done.

Score franks and grill 3 inches from coals 5 to 6 minutes, or until browned, turning frequently (brush with sauce, if used).

Halves, quarters, or large pieces—Grill 5 inches from coals. Fold wing tips back toward cut side. Brush chicken with cooking oil, melted butter, or sauce. Place, cut side down, on greased grill over drip pan. Grill for 20 minutes. Turn and brush with oil or butter; grill 10 to 20 minutes, or until chicken is tender, turning when necessary to prevent charring. When substituting sauce for oil or butter, turn and brush frequently during grilling.

Wing-drum appetizers—Put wing-drums (meatiest portion of each chicken wing), one layer deep, in a hinged basket broiler. Brush with sauce; grill 5 inches from coals for 45 minutes, turning and brushing frequently with sauce.

Using 8-ounce tails, thawed, cut around under-shell and remove. Insert a skewer lengthwise through meat to keep tail flat. Grill, shell-side down, 4 inches from coals 7 minutes, brushing frequently with sauce. Turn and grill 5 minutes, or until tender.

Cut each raw shrimp through shell along back; remove black vein. Carefully spread shell open; rinse and drain well. Marinate several hours or overnight. Put shrimp, one layer deep, in hinged basket broiler. Turning occasionally, grill 3 inches from coals 15 minutes, or until shrimp are done.

Marinades and Sauces

Saucy Roquefort filling—Make a large depression in the center of each burger and fill with 2 teaspoons crumbled Roquefort cheese and ½ teaspoon olive oil. Reshape burgers to seal in filling. Or use bottled barbecue sauce for brushing.

Tomato sauce, see recipe below. Or use either pineapple marinade (see ribs) or bottled barbecue sauce.

Tomato basting sauce—Brown ½ cup chopped onion in 1 tablespoon melted butter. Blend in 1 cup ketchup, ¾ cup cider vinegar, ½ cup water, ½ cup light molasses, 1 envelope garlic salad dressing mix, and 2 beef bouillon cubes; bring to boiling. Simmer 15 minutes. (Vary above recipe by substituting sake for vinegar, and French salad dressing mix for garlic salad dressing mix.) Or use either pineapple marinade (see ribs) or plum sauce below.

Plum sauce—Puree purple plums (17-ounce jar). Mix puree with the plum syrup, ¼ cup cider vinegar, 2 tablespoons finely chopped chutney, 2 tablespoons apricot preserves, and ½ teaspoon salt. Simmer 10 minutes. Or use pineapple marinade (see ribs).

Butter sauce—Heat 1 cup butter, 2 tablespoons lemon juice, ¼ teaspoon salt, ¼ teaspoon paprika, ⅛ teaspoon black pepper, and ¼ cup chopped parsley until butter is melted. Serve remaining sauce hot with the lobster.

Herb marinade—Blend ⅔ cup salad oil, ¾ cup lemon juice, 1 tablespoon prepared horseradish, 1 teaspoon seasoned salt, ⅛ teaspoon cayenne pepper, ½ teaspoon crushed savory, ½ teaspoon crushed tarragon leaves, and 1 large clove garlic, crushed. Mix well before adding shrimp.

BURGERS (beef)

FRANKFURTERS

CHICKEN

ROCK LOBSTER TAILS

SHRIMP

Hot Coffee Cake

Purchase or bake a coffee cake and, if desired, cut into slices and butter slices. Wrap loosely in a double thickness of heavy-duty aluminum foil. Place on one side of the grill about 5 to 7 inches from medium coals. Rotate frequently to heat thoroughly, 12 to 20 minutes depending on size of coffee cake. Turn back foil and serve from package.

SAUCY IDEAS

Chunky Barbecue Sauce

    2 tablespoons butter or margarine
    1 medium onion, chopped
    1 clove garlic, chopped
    ½ cup chopped celery with leaves
    ¼ cup chopped green pepper
    1 can (16 ounces) tomatoes (undrained)
    1 can (6 ounces) tomato paste
    1 bay leaf
    2 teaspoons dry mustard
    1½ teaspoons salt
    ½ teaspoon ground cloves
    ½ teaspoon ground allspice
    ⅓ cup vinegar
    3 tablespoons dark molasses
    2 teaspoons Tabasco
    2 slices lemon

1. Heat butter in a large deep saucepan. Add onion and garlic; cook until onion is tender, but not brown. Add remaining ingredients; simmer 30 minutes, stirring occasionally. Remove from heat; cool. Put through a food mill or sieve, if desired.
2. Use as a brushing sauce for chicken, ribs, frankfurters, or hamburgers during grilling.

About 2¾ cups sauce

Tabasco Butter

    ½ cup butter
    ½ teaspoon Tabasco
    1 tablespoon lime juice

Cream butter with Tabasco and lime juice. Spread over hot grilled steak.

Enough butter for 8 pounds of steak

Note: To serve butter with lobster, melt butter and stir in Tabasco and lime juice.

Orange Basting Sauce

    2 tablespoons light corn syrup
    1 teaspoon garlic salt
    1 teaspoon dry mustard
    ½ teaspoon monosodium glutamate
    ½ cup orange juice
      Few drops Tabasco
    2 tablespoons butter or margarine

1. Mix all ingredients in a small saucepan. Heat until butter is melted; stir to blend.
2. Brush on chicken or pork while sauce is still warm.

About ⅔ cup sauce

Note: If using chicken, coat pieces with cooking oil and let stand about 30 minutes before cooking.

Easy Hamburger Glaze

    ½ cup ketchup
    ¼ cup prepared mustard
    ½ teaspoon Tabasco

1. Combine all ingredients; mixing well.
2. Use to brush on hamburgers during grilling.

About ¾ cup glaze

Mustard Barbecue Sauce

    ½ cup molasses
    ½ cup prepared mustard
    ½ cup cider vinegar

1. Blend molasses and mustard. Add vinegar and mix well.
2. Store tightly covered at room temperature or in the refrigerator. Sauce will keep indefinitely.
3. Use as a brushing sauce when grilling hamburgers, frankfurters, or spareribs.

About 1½ cups sauce

PICNICKING (OUTDOOR PARTIES)

"Three squares" a day may satisfy the body yet leave the spirit hungry. That's especially true during picnic weather, when everyday meals can seem *too* square. Blue skies and green grass make a colorful invitation back to nature where a simple lunch can seem like a party.

Our word "picnic" comes from the French "piquenique": to pick up a trifle. Along with the name, we should also borrow some of that famous French inventiveness with food. Not that picnic menus need to be labored; that would spoil the fun. But if your family knows, even before opening the hamper, that baked beans and deviled eggs are sure to be on the menu, its time to give them a few surprises.

Clever picnics can be set up indoors, in some part of the house not generally used for eating, such as the family or living room. This may be a makeshift picnic, organized as a substitute for the real thing when the weather doesn't cooperate. It's better than disappointing the family, but for most people, a true picnic is not housebound.

Not that you need to go far. The backyard will do just fine, especially if you want to cook part of the meal in the kitchen but eat outdoors. The range and grill are compatible partners, each doing what it does best.

But if what you want is a scenic backdrop for the meal, the beach, hills, or forest are well worth the drive.

So location is flexible. The "picking up" of the meal and the carefree mood are the only essentials. You'll find your own mood growing a lot more carefree as your picnic practice grows.

A little organization and thought beforehand will free you to enjoy your picnic. Confirmed picnickers keep a hamper stocked with basics so that getting underway isn't such a big production.

STOCKING THE PICNIC BASKET

At the bottom: paper bag for cleanup
Paper plates, cups, napkins, and towels
Plastic "silverware" and serving pieces
Salt, pepper
Mustard, ketchup, and other favorite seasonings
At the top: easy-care tablecloth

Notice that the tablecloth is listed last. That's because you'll want it first thing, to set the table, or to create an eating spot on the grass even where there is no table.

PLANNING THE MENU

Since diversion is the point of the picnic, avoid the predictable, try some of the following suggestions, and start a file of your own unusual recipes, especially tailored for transporting and for outdoor eating.

Finger foods are ideal for outdoor meals. Chicken, sandwiches, and ribs all are great main-dish choices. So are such go-withs as potato chips, shoestring potatoes, and chilled vegetables cut julienne style. To make them interesting, bring a plastic container of dip.

Let the four food groups (see chart, page 6) provide your basic menu formula: Meat or other protein food, bread, vegetables and fruits, and a milk drink in the thermos meet all the nutrient needs. Then add that essential ingredient, imagination, to make the menu fun.

FOR SAFETY'S SAKE

To avoid an unhappy aftermath to your picnic, keep hot foods hot and cold foods cold. Use a styrofoam cooler, ice bucket, and thermos to help keep foods at the proper temperatures.

PATIO BRUNCH

Frosty Sours

Orange Juice with Mint Sprigs

Grill-Baked Eggs au Gratin (page 44)

Zucchini Vinaigrette

Hot Buttered Pineapple on the Spit (page 39)

Coffee

Frosty Sours

　1 can (6 ounces) frozen orange juice
　　　concentrate
　2 juice cans water
　1 juice can bourbon
　1 can (5¾ ounces) frozen lemon juice
　2 egg whites (reserve yolks for cheese sauce)
　¼ cup sugar
　　Orange slices
　　Mint sprigs

Combine all ingredients except orange slices and mint sprigs in an electric blender. Blend at low speed until smooth, then at high speed until frothy. Pour into ice-filled glasses. Garnish with orange slices and mint sprigs.

Ten 4-ounce servings

Zucchini Vinaigrette

　5 or 6 medium zucchini
　1 package Italian salad dressing mix
　¼ cup white wine vinegar
　½ cup salad oil
　2 tablespoons finely chopped green pepper
　2 tablespoons finely chopped parsley
　¼ cup finely chopped green onion
　3 tablespoons sweet pickle relish

1. Cut ends from each zucchini and slice lengthwise into 6 pieces. Cook in a small amount of boiling salted water about 3 minutes, or until crisp-tender. Drain if necessary and cool; put into a shallow dish.
2. While zucchini is cooling, combine the remaining ingredients in a jar with a tight-fitting lid. Cover and shake vigorously to mix well.
3. Pour vinaigrette sauce over zucchini. Chill 4 hours or overnight. Serve with Grill-Baked Eggs au Gratin.

About 6 servings

BRUNCH BARBECUE

Pitcher of Sunshine

Mixed Grill (page 23)

Spit-Roasted Canadian Bacon (page 40)

Hot Coffee Cake (page 54)

Pitcher of Sunshine

Mix equal amounts of chilled orange juice (either fresh or reconstituted frozen juice) with chilled champagne or ginger ale. If desired, garnish with orange slices and serve immediately in tall glasses.

BARBECUE DINNER

Ham Steak Barbecue (page 20)

Baked Sweet Potatoes in Foil (page 51)

Orange-Pea Salad

Brownies

Orange-Pea Salad

2 packages (10 ounces each) frozen green
    peas
1⅓ cups chopped celery
½ teaspoon dried leaf tarragon
¼ cup dairy sour cream
2 teaspoons grated orange peel
2 tablespoons thawed frozen orange juice
    concentrate
1 teaspoon salt
½ teaspoon sugar
    Salad greens
    Orange sections

1. Cook peas according to package directions.
Drain and cool. Mix with celery, tarragon, sour
cream, orange peel, orange concentrate, salt, and
sugar. Chill.
2. Line a serving bowl with salad greens, spoon
in pea salad, and garnish with orange sections.

6 servings

Brownies

½ cup butter
2 ounces (2 squares) unsweetened chocolate
2 eggs
1 cup sugar
⅔ cup all-purpose flour
½ teaspoon baking powder
⅛ teaspoon salt
¾ cup pecans, coarsely chopped

1. Melt butter and chocolate together; set aside to
cool.
2. Beat eggs and sugar until thick and piled
softly; add cooled chocolate mixture and beat
until blended.
3. Blend flour, baking powder, and salt; add to
chocolate mixture and mix until blended. Stir in
nuts.
4. Turn batter into a greased 9×9×2-inch baking
pan and spread evenly.
5. Bake at 350°F 35 to 40 minutes. Cool on rack.
Cut into squares.

3 dozen cookies

OUTDOOR FEAST

Fresh Sweet Cherry Appetizer Tray

Spit-Roasted Cornish Hens (page 37)

Savory Rice Pilaf

Tossed Green Salad

Fresh Sweet Cherry Appetizer Tray

Fresh sweet cherries
Assorted cheeses (Cheddar, Swiss, Gouda,
    Kuminost)
Sweet gherkins, thickly sliced
Salami, thinly sliced
Cream cheese
Horseradish
Parsley

1. Wash cherries just before serving and put into
a serving bowl.
2. Cut some of the Cheddar and Swiss cheeses
into ½-inch cubes and put, along with sliced
gherkins, onto party picks. Slice remaining
cheeses.
3. Soften cream cheese at room temperature and
season with a small amount of horseradish.
Spread on salami slices and shape into cornuco-
pias, fastening with wooden picks. Garnish with
parsley.
4. Arrange all appetizers on a large tray with the
cherries.

Savory Rice Pilaf

    2 tablespoons butter or margarine
    ½ cup chopped celery
    ¼ cup chopped onion
    ¼ cup sliced mushrooms
    1 cup uncooked rice
    2½ cups chicken broth
    1 tablespoon soy sauce
    ½ teaspoon salt
    2 tablespoons chopped parsley

1. Heat butter in a saucepan. Add celery, onion, and mushrooms; cook until tender. Stir in rice and brown lightly. Add chicken broth, soy sauce, and salt. Cover and simmer over low heat until liquid is absorbed, about 25 minutes.
2. Before serving, stir in parsley.

6 servings

PATIO DINNER

Orange-Glazed Pork Loin (page 24)

Kettle Patio Potatoes (page 51)

Vegetable Medley

Sour Cream Slaw

Ice Cream Sundaes

Vegetable Medley

    ½ cup butter
    2 cups (about ½ pound) sliced zucchini
    1 cup chopped green pepper
    1 cup chopped celery
    ¾ cup thinly sliced onion
    2 cups cubed eggplant
    ½ teaspoon salt
    1 cup coarse bread crumbs
    3 medium tomatoes, sliced

1. Heat butter in a skillet. Add zucchini, green pepper, celery, and onion; sauté until just tender. Stir in eggplant and salt; spoon into a buttered 2-quart shallow casserole, leaving butter in skillet. Add crumbs to butter in skillet. Top vegetables with tomato slices and buttered crumbs.
2. Bake at 350°F about 30 minutes.

About 8 servings

Sour Cream Slaw

    ¾ cup dairy sour cream
    1 tablespoon vinegar
    ½ teaspoon dill weed
    ½ teaspoon salt
    ⅛ teaspoon pepper
    5 cups shredded cabbage (red and green)
    ½ cup chopped green pepper

1. Gently blend sour cream, vinegar, dill weed, salt, and pepper in a small bowl. Cover and chill.
2. When ready to serve, toss cabbage and green pepper lightly with sour cream dressing.

About 8 servings

RIB AND CORN ROAST

Barbecued Spareribs à la Marinade (page 20)

Corn on the Grill (page 50)

Bacon-Bean Salad

Garlic Bread (page 50)

Fresh Fruit

Bacon-Bean Salad

    ⅔ cup cider vinegar
    ¾ cup sugar
    1 teaspoon salt
    1 can (16 ounces) cut green beans
    1 can (16 ounces) cut wax beans
    1 can (16 ounces) kidney beans, thoroughly
        rinsed and drained
    1 can (16 ounces) lima beans
    1 medium onion, quartered and finely sliced
    1 medium green pepper, chopped
    ½ teaspoon freshly ground black pepper
    ⅓ cup salad oil
    1 pound bacon, cut in 1-inch squares

1. Blend vinegar, sugar, and salt in a small saucepan. Heat until the sugar is dissolved. Remove from heat and set aside.
2. Drain all beans and toss with onion, green pepper, vinegar mixture, and the pepper. Pour oil over all and toss to coat evenly. Store in a large covered container in refrigerator.

3. When ready to serve, fry bacon until crisp; drain on absorbent paper. Toss the bacon with bean mixture.

About 12 servings

Note: If desired, omit bacon.

FISH BAKE

Creamy Shrimp Dip

Picnic Green Pea Soup

Savory Outdoor Baked Fish (page 44)

French Fries in a Poke (page 51)

Cookout Lemon Cake

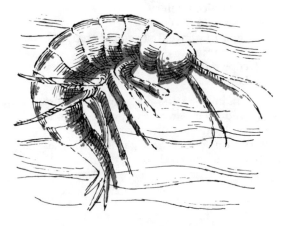

Creamy Shrimp Dip

1 package (8 ounces) cream cheese, softened
1 can (10¾ ounces) condensed cream of
    shrimp soup
2 tablespoons chopped green onion
1 teaspoon lemon juice
¼ teaspoon curry powder
    Dash garlic powder
4 drops Tabasco
    Raw vegetables

1. Combine cream cheese, soup, green onion, lemon juice, curry powder, garlic powder, and

Tabasco with a beater just until blended; do not overbeat. Chill.
2. Serve as a dip with raw vegetable pieces.

About 2½ cups dip

Picnic Green Pea Soup

2 tablespoons chopped onion
¼ cup sliced celery
1 tablespoon butter or margarine
1 can (11¼ ounces) condensed green pea
    soup
1 soup-can water
1 can (8 ounces) tomatoes, drained and
    chopped
    Thyme croutons

1. Cook onion and celery in butter until tender. Blend in soup; gradually add water, stirring constantly. Add tomatoes and heat, stirring occasionally.
2. Garnish with croutons.

About 3 servings

Thyme Croutons: Cut 1 slice white bread into cubes. Heat 2 tablespoons butter or margarine in a skillet; add bread cubes and brown them, stirring constantly. Add a dash of ground thyme.

Cookout Lemon Cake

1 package (about 19 ounces) yellow cake mix
2 teaspoons grated lemon peel
¾ cup sugar
1 tablespoon lemon juice
½ cup melted butter

1. Prepare cake mix according to package directions, adding 1 teaspoon lemon peel. Turn into 2 well-greased 9-inch round pans.
2. Combine sugar with remaining lemon peel and spoon over batter in pans.
3. Combine lemon juice and butter. Pour over sugar.
4. Bake at 350°F about 30 minutes, or until cake tests done. Cake will have a crispy golden brown top.
5. Cool on racks. Leave cake in pans and wrap in foil to carry to cookout. If the day is cool, set pan on grill to warm over the coals before serving.

Two 9-inch cake layers

onion and cook until lightly browned, stirring occasionally.

2. Blend flour, sugar, dry mustard, and garlic powder. Stir into mixture in saucepan along with chili sauce, water, vinegar, and Worcestershire sauce. Bring to boiling; boil 1 to 2 minutes, stirring constantly.

3. Add frankfurters to sauce; cover and simmer until franks are heated thoroughly.

4. Brush buns with some of the sauce; toast under broiler or on grill. Serve frankfurters in buns and, if desired, spoon on additional sauce.

24 servings

PATIO PICNIC

Iron-Pot Barbecued Franks

Patio Picnic Bean Salad

Sparkling Peach Salad

Mansion Dessert Squares

Iron-Pot Barbecued Franks

¾ cup butter
1 cup minced onion
½ cup all-purpose flour
1½ teaspoons sugar
1 teaspoon dry mustard
½ teaspoon garlic powder
1½ cups chili sauce
1½ cups water
½ cup cider vinegar
¼ cup Worcestershire sauce
24 frankfurters
24 frankfurter buns

1. Heat butter in a large saucepot or kettle; add

Patio Picnic Bean Salad

4 cans (15 ounces each) kidney beans, drained
8 hard-cooked eggs, diced
1 cup chopped onion
2 cups diced celery
1⅓ cups pickle relish
2 cups (8 ounces) shredded sharp Cheddar cheese
2 cups dairy sour cream
Lettuce

1. Mix kidney beans, eggs, onion, celery, pickle relish, and cheese in a large bowl. Add sour cream and toss lightly together; chill.

2. Serve on lettuce and garnish with additional hard-cooked egg, if desired.

About 20 servings

Sparkling Peach Salad

6 cups ginger ale
3 envelopes unflavored gelatin
2 cans (17 ounces each) sliced peaches, drained
2 tablespoons finely chopped crystallized ginger

1. Pour 1 cup of ginger ale into a small saucepan. Sprinkle gelatin over it. Stir over low heat until gelatin is dissolved. Stir gelatin into remaining ginger ale.

2. Chill gelatin until slightly thicker than consis-

tency of thick unbeaten egg white. Mix in peaches and ginger. Turn into a 9-inch square pan and chill until firm. Cut into squares.

16 servings

Mansion Dessert Squares

1¾ cups all-purpose flour
1 teaspoon baking powder
¼ teaspoon baking soda
¼ teaspoon salt
1 cup butter
2 teaspoons vanilla extract
1½ cups firmly packed light brown sugar
2 eggs
1 package (12 ounces) semisweet chocolate pieces

1. Blend flour, baking powder, baking soda, and salt; set aside.
2. Cream butter with vanilla extract. Add brown sugar gradually, creaming until fluffy. Add eggs, one at a time, beating thoroughly after each addition.
3. Mix in the dry ingredients. Stir in chocolate pieces. Turn into two greased 9-inch square baking pans.

4. Bake at 350°F 30 to 35 minutes. Cut into squares.

18 servings

CHOWDER BEACH PARTY

Pacific Seafood Chowder

Northwest Fruit Slaw

Buttered Crusty Bread

Frosted Spice Cake

Pacific Seafood Chowder

1½ pounds North Pacific halibut, fresh or frozen
1 can (7½ ounces) Alaska King crab or 1 package (6 ounces) frozen Alaska King crab
3 medium potatoes
1 large sweet Spanish onion
¾ cup chopped celery
¼ cup chopped green pepper
2 cloves garlic, minced
¼ cup butter or margarine
2 cans (16 ounces each) tomatoes
2 cups clam-tomato juice
1½ teaspoons salt
¼ teaspoon pepper
¼ teaspoon thyme
¼ teaspoon marjoram
1 dozen small hard-shell clams
Snipped parsley

1. Defrost halibut, if frozen. Cut into 1-inch chunks. Drain canned crab and slice. Or defrost, drain, and slice frozen crab. Pare potatoes and cut into ½-inch pieces. Peel and thinly slice onion.
2. Sauté onion, celery, green pepper, and garlic in butter in a saucepot. Add tomatoes with liquid, clam-tomato juice, and seasonings. Cover and simmer 30 minutes. Add halibut, potatoes, and clams. Cover and simmer about 10 minutes, or until halibut and potatoes are done and clam shells open. Add crab and heat through.
3. Sprinkle with parsley. Serve with buttered crusty bread.

About 8 servings

Northwest Fruit Slaw

    1 can (16 ounces) light sweet cherries
    1 can (16 ounces) dark sweet cherries
    3 fresh Anjou, Bosc, or Comice pears
    2 cups finely shredded cabbage
      Creamy Fruit Mayonnaise
      Lettuce

1. Drain cherries and remove pits. Reserve a few cherries for garnish. Core and dice 1 pear. Core and slice remaining pears into wedges for garnish.
2. Combine cabbage, cherries, and diced pear. Add Creamy Fruit Mayonnaise and toss lightly to coat fruit and cabbage.
3. Line a serving bowl with lettuce and spoon in salad. Garnish with pear wedges and reserved cherries.

About 8 servings

Creamy Fruit Mayonnaise

    ⅓ cup mayonnaise
    ⅓ cup dairy sour cream
    1 tablespoon honey
    1 tablespoon lemon juice
    1 tablespoon orange juice
    ¼ teaspoon salt

Combine mayonnaise, sour cream, honey, juices, and salt, blending well.

About ¾ cup fruit mayonnaise

Frosted Spice Cake

    3 cups sifted cake flour
    1½ teaspoons baking powder
    ¾ teaspoon baking soda
    ¾ teaspoon salt
    1½ teaspoons ground cinnamon
    ¾ teaspoon ground nutmeg
    ½ teaspoon ground allspice
    ½ teaspoon ground cloves
    ¾ cup butter or margarine
    1 cup firmly packed light brown sugar
    1 cup sugar
    3 eggs
    1½ cups buttermilk
      Caramel Frosting
      Walnut halves

1. Sift flour, baking powder, baking soda, salt, and spices together; set aside.
2. Beat butter until softened. Add sugar gradually, creaming until fluffy after each addition. Add eggs, one at a time, beating thoroughly after each addition.
3. Beating only until smooth after each addition, alternately add dry ingredients in fourths and buttermilk in thirds to creamed mixture. Turn batter into a greased 13×9×2-inch pan and spread evenly.
4. Bake at 350°F 40 to 45 minutes, or until cake tests done with a cake tester or wooden pick. Place on a rack and cool completely in pan.
5. Frost with Caramel Frosting and decorate with walnut halves.

1 frosted 13×9-inch cake

Caramel Frosting

    ½ cup butter
    1 cup firmly packed brown sugar
    ¼ cup half-and-half
    1½ cups sifted confectioners' sugar

1. Melt butter in a heavy skillet over low heat. Blend in brown sugar and half-and-half. Stirring constantly, bring to boiling and cook 1 minute, or until sugar is completely dissolved.
2. Remove from heat and cool to lukewarm (110°F)
3. When syrup has cooled, gradually add confectioners' sugar, beating until blended after each addition. If necessary, continue beating until thick enough to spread.

1½ cups frosting

APPETIZERS

On-the-Wing Appetizers

  30 chicken wing-drums (2½ to 3½ pounds)
  ½ teaspoon salt
  ¼ cup soy sauce
  ¼ cup spiced peach syrup
  2 tablespoons sugar
  ¼ teaspoon monosodium glutamate
  ½ teaspoon ground ginger
  1 tablespoon lemon juice
  5 drops Tabasco
  1 clove garlic, crushed

1. Disjoint the wings; use thickest wing portions for appetizers and remaining wing portions for chicken broth.
2. Place the wing-drums on rack on a foil-lined baking sheet or broiler pan; sprinkle with salt.
3. Mix remaining ingredients thoroughly; brush marinade generously on wing-drums.
4. Bake at 350°F about 1 hour, or until wing drums are golden brown and tender, brushing frequently with the marinade. Cool.
5. For easy toting to the picnic, pile appetizers into a casserole with a cover.

About 10 servings

Mustard Dipping Sauce

  ⅔ cup mayonnaise
  ½ cup prepared mustard
  ¼ cup bottled steak sauce
    Juice of 1 lemon
  10 drops Tabasco

1. Mix all ingredients well in a chilled bowl.
2. Use as a dip for chilled lobster or crab meat; crisp raw vegetables; or hot appetizers, such as Vienna sausages or cocktail sausages, bite size pieces of cooked frankfurters, or luncheon meat served on cocktail picks.

About 1⅓ cups sauce

Tomato-Cheese Dip

  1 package (8 ounces) cream cheese, softened
  1 medium ripe tomato, peeled and cut in small pieces
  ¾ teaspoon salt
  1 teaspoon grated onion
  1 or 2 drops Tabasco
    Carrot and celery sticks

1. With a fork, thoroughly blend cream cheese and tomato in a bowl. Mix in salt, onion, and Tabasco. Chill.
2. Serve with celery and carrot sticks for dippers.

About 2 cups dip

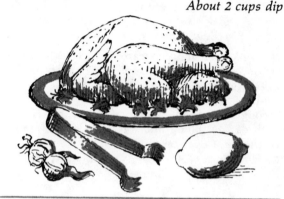

MAIN DISHES

Crunchy Peanut Chicken

  ⅓ cup all-purpose flour
  ½ teaspoon salt
  ¼ teaspoon pepper
  1 broiler-fryer chicken (2½ to 3 pounds), cut in pieces
  1 egg
  2 tablespoons milk
  1 cup finely chopped dry roasted peanuts
  ½ cup butter, melted

1. Combine flour, salt, and pepper; coat chicken pieces evenly.
2. Beat egg and milk together. Dip chicken in egg mixture, then coat with peanuts.
3. Put pieces skin-side up in a 13×9×2-inch baking pan. Pour butter over chicken.
4. Bake at 400°F 1 hour, or until chicken is tender. Remove from oven. Cool slightly at room temperature; refrigerate.

About 4 servings

Stuffed Frankfurter and Macaroni Casserole

   2 cups elbow macaroni
1½ cups shredded Cheddar cheese
   ½ cup finely chopped onion
1½ cups milk
   1 tablespoon prepared mustard
   ½ teaspoon caraway seed
   6 frankfurters
     Chopped pimento-stuffed olives, sweet
        pickle relish, ketchup, or chili sauce
     Shredded Cheddar cheese

1. Cook and drain macaroni. Mix with cheese, onion, milk, mustard, and caraway seed. Turn into a greased 1½-quart shallow casserole. Slit franks lengthwise without cutting all the way through. Arrange on top of macaroni. Fill slits with desired filling and top with desired amount of cheese. Cover casserole tightly.
2. Heat in a 350°F oven 30 minutes. Remove cover and heat 10 minutes.

6 servings

Flavor-Rich Baked Beans

   2 cans (about 16 ounces each) baked beans
        in tomato sauce
   1 cup gingersnap crumbs
   ¼ cup ketchup

   2 tablespoons molasses
   1 tablespoon instant minced onion
   ½ teaspoon seasoned salt
   3 bacon slices

1. Mix baked beans, gingersnap crumbs, ketchup, molasses, onion, and seasoned salt. Turn into greased 1-quart casserole: Top with the bacon slices.
2. Heat in a 375°F oven 15 to 20 minutes, or until thoroughly heated. If desired, set under broiler to crisp bacon.

8 servings

Dilly-Bacon Stuffed Eggs

   12 hard-cooked eggs
    1 package (3 ounces) cream cheese, softened
    ½ cup dairy sour cream
    ½ teaspoon dill weed
    1 tablespoon capers
   10 to 12 slices bacon, diced and cooked

1. Cut each egg into halves crosswise or lengthwise. Remove egg yolks and mash with a fork.
2. Beat cream cheese until fluffy; mix in egg yolks, sour cream, dill weed, capers, and bacon pieces.
3. Generously fill egg whites with mixture. Chill thoroughly.
4. If desired, garnish each egg half with a sprig of watercress.

24 stuffed egg halves

FILLINGS FOR SANDWICHES

Blend ingredients thoroughly before preparing sandwiches. Spread desired bread with butter, margarine, or mayonnaise and then with filling. Each filling is enough for 4 sandwiches. To serve, cut into attractive shapes.

Baked Bean

   1 cup drained canned baked beans with
        tomato sauce
   ⅓ cup chopped sweet pickle
   2 tablespoons ketchup or chili sauce
   1 tablespoon minced onion

Bologna

¾ cup ground bologna
1 hard-cooked egg, finely chopped
2 to 3 tablespoons chili sauce
2 tablespoons salad dressing or mayonnaise
1 teaspoon prepared horseradish
¼ teaspoon salt

Cheddar Cheese

¾ cup finely shredded Cheddar cheese
½ cup finely chopped corned beef
2 tablespoons chopped sweet pickle
1 tablespoon chopped pimento
1 teaspoon prepared mustard
¼ teaspoon onion salt

Citrus Special

½ cup peanut butter
¼ cup orange juice
1 teaspoon grated orange peel
⅓ cup shredded or flaked coconut

Deviled Ham-Raisin

1 can (4½ ounces) deviled ham
½ cup chopped celery
¼ cup chopped pecans
¼ cup chopped raisins
2 tablespoons mayonnaise

Egg Salad

4 hard-cooked eggs, chopped
2 tablespoons chopped pimento-stuffed
   olives
2 tablespoons mayonnaise
½ teaspoon dry mustard
½ teaspoon salt
   Few grains pepper

Favorite Fish

¾ cup cooked fish (salmon, tuna, crab meat,
   or shrimp), flaked or finely chopped
½ cup finely chopped cabbage
3 tablespoons chopped ripe olives
3 tablespoons salad dressing or mayonnaise
1 tablespoon olive liquid (from can)
¼ teaspoon paprika
2 or 3 drops of Tabasco

Ham and Cheese Supreme

¾ cup creamy cottage cheese
⅓ cup (about 3 ounces) deviled ham
¼ cup salted peanuts (skins removed),
   chopped
2 tablespoons salad dressing or mayonnaise
1 tablespoon prepared horseradish
1 teaspoon chopped chives

Ham-Pineapple

½ cup ground cooked ham
½ cup well-drained crushed pineapple
3 tablespoons salad dressing or mayonnaise
2 teaspoons brown sugar

Hungry Man's Choice

1 cup (about 8 ounces) chopped canned
   luncheon meat, minced cooked ham, or
   minced roast beef
¼ cup chopped garlic dill pickle
2 to 3 tablespoons salad dressing or
   mayonnaise

Liver Sausage

6 ounces Braunschweiger (smoked liver
   sausage)
¼ cup drained pickle relish
2 tablespoons grated onion

Picnic Green Pea Soup; Creamy Shrimp Dip;
Savory Outdoor Baked Fish; Cookout Lemon Cake;
French Fries in a Poke

Olive-Pecan

1 package (3 ounces) cream cheese, softened
⅓ cup chopped green olives
¼ cup salted pecans, finely chopped
1 to 2 tablespoons milk
1 or 2 drops Tabasco
Few grains salt

Salami-Kidney Bean

½ cup finely chopped salami (about 4 ounces)
½ cup drained canned kidney beans, chopped
2 to 3 tablespoons chili sauce
1 teaspoon minced onion
1 teaspoon prepared mustard

Special Chicken

1 cup minced cooked chicken
¼ cup finely chopped celery
4 to 6 pitted ripe olives, chopped
2 teaspoons minced parsley
3 tablespoons dairy sour cream
¼ teaspoon salt
Few grains pepper

Tuna Salad

1 cup (6½- or 7-ounce can) tuna, drained
   and flaked
⅓ cup chopped celery
1 tablespoon chopped sweet pickle
1 tablespoon chopped onion
¼ cup mayonnaise
½ teaspoon salt

SALADS

All-Seasons Macaroni Salad

1 cup dairy sour cream
½ cup Italian salad dressing
½ teaspoon salt
¼ teaspoon seasoned salt
   Few grains pepper
2 cups (8 ounces) elbow macaroni, cooked
   and drained
1½ cups diced cooked chicken
½ pound bacon, panbroiled and crumbled
2 hard-cooked eggs, chopped
¼ cup chopped pimento
1 large tomato, diced
2 tablespoons lemon juice
1 avocado, peeled and sliced
   Curly endive

1. Mix together in a bowl the sour cream, salad dressing, salts, and pepper; add macaroni and chicken and mix well. Chill thoroughly.
2. Add bacon, eggs, pimento, and tomato to macaroni; toss lightly. Turn into salad bowl.
3. Sprinkle lemon juice over avocado slices. Garnish salad with avocado and endive. Additional bacon, chicken, eggs, pimento, and tomato may be used to garnish, if desired.

6 servings

Blue Ribbon Potato-Onion Salad

2 pounds potatoes (about 6 medium),
   cooked and peeled
2½ tablespoons cider vinegar
1 tablespoon salad oil
1½ teaspoons salt
3 hard-cooked eggs, chopped
1 cup diced celery
1¾ cups dairy sour cream
½ teaspoon sugar
   Few grains pepper
2 tablespoons cider vinegar
1½ teaspoons prepared mustard
½ cup grated onion (or blender puréed)
½ cup sliced ripe olives

1. Cut potatoes into ½-inch cubes and put into a bowl. Toss with a mixture of vinegar, oil, and salt. Add eggs, celery, and dressing; toss until mixed. Cover and chill thoroughly.

2. Combine remaining ingredients. Chill until ready to use.

3. Turn salad into a chilled salad bowl.

10 to 12 servings

Kidney Bean-Mushroom Salad

  2 cans (about 15 ounces each) kidney beans,
      drained and rinsed
  2 cans or jars (4 or 4½ ounces each) sliced
      mushrooms, drained
  1 to 1½ cups thinly sliced celery (cut
      diagonally)
  ½ cup golden raisins
  ¼ cup red wine vinegar
  1 clove garlic, minced
  4 drops Tabasco
  ½ teaspoon ground cardamom
  ½ teaspoon curry powder
  ½ teaspoon tarragon leaves, crushed
  ¼ cup olive oil or other salad oil

1. Combine kidney beans, mushrooms, celery, and raisins in a large bowl; toss lightly.

2. Pour vinegar into a bottle and add remaining ingredients. Cover and shake vigorously. Pour over vegetables and toss lightly until well mixed. Chill until ready to pack for the picnic.

3. If desired, sprinkle flaked or shredded coconut over salad before serving.

8 to 10 servings

DESSERTS

Frosted Chocolate Drop Cookies

  2½ cups sifted all-purpose flour
   ½ cup cocoa
   1 teaspoon baking powder
   1 teaspoon baking soda
   ½ teaspoon salt
   1 cup butter
   1 teaspoon vanilla extract
  1¾ cups sugar
   1 cup creamy cottage cheese
   2 eggs
   ½ cup chopped pecans

1. Sift flour, cocoa, baking powder, baking soda, and salt together; set aside.

2. Cream butter with vanilla extract. Add sugar gradually, beating until light and fluffy. Add cottage cheese and beat thoroughly. Add eggs, one at a time, beating well after each addition.

3. Add dry ingredients gradually to creamed mixture, beating until blended. Stir in pecans.

4. Drop by rounded teaspoonfuls onto buttered cookie sheets.

5. Bake at 350°F about 15 minutes. Place cookies on a rack to cool. Spread Butter Frosting on cooled cookies.

About 8 dozen cookies

Butter Frosting

  2½ cups confectioners' sugar
  ¼ cup butter, softened
  ¼ cup milk
  1 teaspoon vanilla extract

Combine confectioners' sugar, butter, milk, and vanilla extract in a small bowl; beat until smooth.

About 1½ cups frosting

Apricot Butter Bars

1 cup sifted all-purpose flour
¼ cup sugar
½ cup butter
⅓ cup sifted all-purpose flour
½ teaspoon baking powder
½ teaspoon salt
2 eggs
1 teaspoon vanilla extract
1 cup firmly packed brown sugar
1 cup dried apricots, snipped
½ to ¾ cup walnuts, chopped

1. Mix 1 cup flour and the sugar in a bowl. Cut in the butter with a pastry blender or two knives until the particles formed are the size of small peas. Turn into a 9×9×2-inch baking pan and press firmly into an even layer over bottom of pan.
2. Bake at 350°F 25 minutes.
3. Meanwhile, blend remaining ⅓ cup flour, the baking powder, and salt. Set aside.
4. Beat eggs with extract. Add the brown sugar gradually, beating until thick. Stir in the flour mixture, apricots, and nuts.
5. Remove pan from oven; turn the apricot mixture onto the layer in pan and spread evenly.
6. Return to oven and continue baking 30 minutes.
7. Cool completely on a wire rack before cutting into bars.

About 2 dozen cookies

Peanut Blonde Brownies

½ cup chunk-style peanut butter
¼ cup butter or margarine
1 teaspoon vanilla extract
1 cup firmly packed light brown sugar
2 eggs
½ cup sifted all-purpose flour
1 cup chopped salted peanuts
Confectioners' sugar

1. Cream peanut butter with butter and extract. Gradually add brown sugar, beating well. Add eggs, one at a time, beating until fluffy after each addition.
2. Add flour in halves, mixing until blended after each addition. Stir in peanuts. Turn into a greased 8×8×2-inch baking pan and spread evenly.
3. Bake at 350°F 30 to 35 minutes.

4. Remove pan to wire rack to cool 5 minutes before cutting into 2-inch squares. Remove from pan and cool on rack. Sift confectioners' sugar over tops.

16 cookies

Chocolate Cupcakes

½ cup milk
2 to 2½ ounces (2 to 2½ squares) unsweetened chocolate
1 egg, slightly beaten
¼ cup sugar
1½ cups sifted cake flour
1¼ teaspoons baking powder
¼ teaspoon baking soda
⅛ teaspoon salt
½ cup butter or margarine
1 teaspoon vanilla extract
1 cup sugar
2 eggs, well beaten
½ cup dairy sour cream

1. Combine milk and chocolate in top of double boiler. Set over simmering water until milk is scalded and chocolate is melted. Stir until well blended.
2. Vigorously stir about 3 tablespoons of the hot milk mixture into the slightly beaten egg; immediately blend into mixture in double boiler. Cook 3 to 5 minutes, stirring constantly. Stir in the ¼ cup sugar.
3. Cook over simmering water about 5 minutes, stirring constantly. Remove from water and set aside to cool.
4. Sift flour, baking powder, baking soda, and salt together; set aside.
5. Cream butter with extract. Add the 1 cup sugar gradually, creaming until fluffy after each addition.
6. Add beaten eggs in thirds, beating thoroughly after each addition. Blend in the cooled chocolate mixture.
7. Beating only until smooth after each addition, alternately add dry ingredients in thirds and sour cream in halves to creamed mixture. Line 2½-inch muffin-pan wells with paper baking cups, or grease wells. Fill each well about one half full with batter.
8. Bake at 350°F 20 to 25 minutes, or until cakes test done.
9. Remove from pans. Cool.
10. Frost, if desired, with Satiny Peanut Butter Frosting.

About 2 dozen cupcakes

Satiny Peanut Butter Frosting

¼ cup peanut butter
¼ cup half-and-half
1 cup (about half a 16-ounce can)
    ready-to-spread vanilla-flavored frosting

Thoroughly mix peanut butter and half-and-half in a bowl until blended. Spoon in frosting while continuing to mix.

About 1½ cups frosting

BEVERAGES

Tomato-Lime Cocktail on the Rocks

3½ cups tomato juice
2 tablespoons lime juice
1 teaspoon Worcestershire sauce
¼ teaspoon Angostura bitters
8 drops Tabasco
4 teaspoons sugar
½ teaspoon seasoned salt

1. Mix all ingredients in a pitcher. Chill thoroughly.
2. Serve over ice cubes in glasses. Garnish each serving, if desired, with a thin slice of lime.

About 1 quart cocktail

Iced Tea

For each serving, prepare 1 cup double-strength tea. Fill tall glasses to brim with crushed ice or ice cubes. Strain tea while hot and pour over ice. Serve with any of the following: thin slices or wedges of lemon, orange, or lime; lemon, orange, or lime juice; sprigs of fresh mint; loaf sugar or sugar syrup; Fruit Kabobs.

Fruit Kabobs: Cut a ½-inch slice from 1 fresh pineapple. Pare the slice and remove "eyes." Using a sharp knife, remove and discard core section. Cut remaining ring into wedges. Cut a ½-inch slice from center of 1 large orange. Cut slice into wedge-shaped pieces. Thread onto each stirrer 1 fresh strawberry, rinsed and hulled; 1 slice lime; 1 red maraschino cherry, well drained; 2 mint leaves; rinsed; 1 large seedless grape, rinsed and stemmed; 1 wedge of the pineapple, and 1 wedge of the orange slice. Chill. Place a kabob in each glass of iced tea before serving.

Lemonade

2 cups lemon juice
6 cups cold water
1½ cups sugar

1. Mix ingredients until sugar is dissolved. Chill thoroughly.
2. Stir lemonade and pour over ice cubes or crushed ice in tall glasses.

About 2 quarts lemonade

Limeade

Follow recipe for Lemonade, substituting lime juice for lemon juice.

Orangeade

Follow recipe for Lemonade, using 6 cups orange juice and decreasing lemon juice to ¼ cup and water to 2 cups.

Cantaloupe Cooler

4 cups diced ripe cantaloupe
½ cup sugar
  Few grains salt
6 tablespoons lime juice
3 cups pineapple-grapefruit juice drink

1. Using an electric blender, liquefy cantaloupe. Pour into a pitcher and add remaining ingredients. Mix well; chill thoroughly.
2. To serve, stir and pour into glasses half-filled with crushed ice. If desired, garnish with sprigs of fresh mint.

1½ quarts cooler

Pineapple Milk Treat

2 cups cold milk
3 tablespoons brown sugar
1 teaspoon vanilla extract
1 cup pineapple chunks, fresh or canned

Put milk, brown sugar, and vanilla extract into an electric blender container. Cover and turn on motor. Add pineapple chunks gradually; blend about 45 seconds, or until thoroughly mixed.

About 3 cups or three 8-ounce servings

Banana Milk Drink

3 or 4 large bananas with brown-flecked peel
2 tablespoons sugar
2 teaspoons vanilla extract
4 cups cold milk

Peel and mash bananas. Blend in sugar and vanilla extract. Stir in milk. Beat vigorously until thoroughly blended.

About 6 servings

Orange Milk Drink

Follow recipe for Banana Milk Drink. Substitute 1½ cups orange juice and 1 tablespoon lemon juice for bananas. Increase sugar to 3 tablespoons. Omit extract. Decrease milk to 3 cups and stir into juices and sugar mixture. Do not beat.

Peanut Butter Milk Drink

Follow recipe for Banana Milk Drink. Substitute ½ cup peanut butter for bananas. Mix ½ cup milk with peanut butter, sugar, and vanilla extract; beat until smooth. Beat in remaining milk.

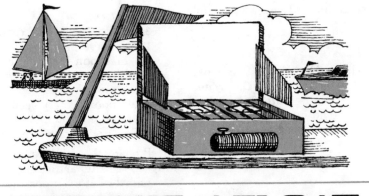

COOKING AFLOAT

When it's vacation time, you want a place in the sun, not down in the galley. So plan meals afloat that will add to, not subtract from, your fun.

FOOD FOR A SHORT SAIL

What to serve on board depends on the length of your trip. If you're just off for an afternoon or evening, you'll probably prepare the food at home and treat the outing much like a picnic. See Picnicking chapter, page 55, for ideas.

Even for longer trips, many dishes can be cooked at home to provide several day's worth of meals. Large cuts of meat, such as beef brisket and corned beef, furnish main dish and sandwich fixings for two or three days. Portable desserts such as pan cakes and brownies are nice to bring on board, too.

FOOD FOR A LONGER TRIP

The galley space in your craft will determine the amount of cooking you can do on board. If you have, say, a sloop or houseboat, you can tackle more ambitious menus than on a smaller sailboat where a picnic lunch works best.

EQUIPMENT

Basic equipment for sailors is the much same as for campers (see page 79). Be sure that cooking pans are rustproof; it pays to buy stainless steel. Storage containers for food should be waterproof.

A utensil much praised by sailors is the pressure cooker. The locking lid makes it safe to use when under way. And since it reduces cooking time, it means an appreciable saving in fuel.

STOVES FOR SAILORS

If you dock at a marina that provides it, you can cook with electricity. That means you can use a hot plate, electric skillet, electric coffee pot, or any electric appliance on board if the power is available. Under way, you'll have to make use of some other fuel, such as alcohol or propane gas.

Alcohol fire is easiest to extinguish, so is preferred by some for safety reasons. Fire is the biggest hazard on board a boat, and it's essential to have a fire extinguisher near the cooking area.

A boat stove should have a guard railing around it to keep pans in place. For this reason, your camper stove shouldn't double as a sailing stove. Pot holders, reaching from the guard rail to the cooking pots, will keep pots in place. When cooking while the boat is in motion, gimbals keep the stove on a level keel. These are accessories that can be purchased from your boat supply store. If your galley has an oven, you can give a lift to meals with hot breads and cakes.

MEAL PLANNING

Plan meals to include the basic four food groups (see chart, page 6) and to make maximum use of convenience foods. After all, this is your vacation! Weight is not the problem that it can be when camping, so canned goods are great to have on board. You will probably put into shore frequently, so plan to buy meat and produce along the way. Canned goods and staples should be stocked in advance of the trip. The well-organized galley keeper makes an inventory of all goods and where they are stowed.

PREPARATION

Cooking afloat has much in common with camper cooking, but there are differences, too. The sailor-cook must secure food and equipment with extra care. Before leaving shore, everything in the galley must be fast. A rough toss from the wake of a passing boat can send things flying, so latch all lockers tightly.

CLEANUP

To keep things shipshape, clean up as you cook, so there's little to do after the meal. Dishwater from lake or ocean works fine, although dishes washed in salt water should be dried at once. If you can spare fresh water, rinse glasses in it before drying.

SOUP AND SANDWICH SEAFARER

Submarine Sandwich

Outrigger Chicken Soup

Crisp Vegetable Relishes

Date-Nut Cupcakes

Lemonade   *Coffee*

Submarine Sandwich

1 long loaf French bread
  Butter or margarine
  Coleslaw (see recipe)
  Thuringer cervelat sausage or pastrami
    slices
  Process American cheese or sharp Cheddar
    slices, halved diagonally
  Tomato slices

1. Slice the bread into halves lengthwise. Spread cut surfaces of both halves with butter or margarine. Set top half aside. Cover bottom half with a generous layer of coleslaw.
2. On the coleslaw, alternate and overlap cervelat or pastrami slices (folded), cheese, and tomato slices. Cover with top of loaf.
3. Insert skewers to hold sandwich together. Cut into serving-size portions.

1 sandwich loaf

Coleslaw

3 to 4 cups shredded cabbage
1 cup mayonnaise
1 tablespoon lemon juice
1 tablespoon cider vinegar
1 tablespoon sugar
2 teaspoons celery seed
¼ teaspoon salt
  Few grains cayenne pepper

1. Prepare the cabbage and chill. Blend remaining ingredients and chill.
2. Shortly before preparing sandwich, pour just enough of the dressing over the cabbage to moisten. Toss lightly until cabbage is well coated.

Outrigger Chicken Soup

1 can (19 ounces) chunky chicken soup
1 hard-cooked egg, chopped
1 tablespoon sweet pickle relish

Combine all ingredients in a saucepan. Heat thoroughly; stir occasionally.

About 2½ cups

Date-Nut Cupcakes

2¼ cups sifted all-purpose flour
2 teaspoons baking powder
¼ teaspoon salt
1 teaspoon ground allspice
1 teaspoon ground cinnamon
¾ cup butter or margarine
½ teaspoon vanilla extract
2 cups sugar
4 egg yolks, well beaten
1 cup unseasoned mashed potatoes
½ cup milk
3 cups (about 12 ounces) coarsely chopped
  pecans
3 cups (about 21 ounces) finely cut date
  pieces
4 egg whites

1. Line 24 2½-inch muffin-pan wells with paper baking cups, or grease well.
2. Sift together 2 cups flour, baking powder, salt, allspice, and cinnamon.

3. Cream butter with vanilla extract. Gradually add sugar, creaming until fluffy. Add egg yolks in thirds, beating thoroughly after each addition.

4. Add mashed potatoes and beat until well blended.

5. Beating only until blended after each addition, add dry ingredients in thirds and milk in halves to creamed mixture; do not overbeat.

6. Put nuts and dates into a large bowl and mix with remaining flour. Pour batter over date-nut mixture and mix thoroughly.

7. Beat egg whites until rounded peaks are formed. Spread over batter and fold together.

8. Spoon batter into muffin pans.

9. Bake at 350°F about 20 minutes, or until a pick inserted in cake comes out clean.

2 dozen cupcakes

SOUP AND SALAD MATEYS

New Orleans Bowl

Roquefort-Vegetable Salad

Melba Toast

Chocolate Coconut Chews   *Fruit Tray*

Iced Lemon Tea   *Iced Coffee*

New Orleans Bowl

1 can (10½ ounces) condensed chicken gumbo
1 can (10½ ounces) condensed chicken-with-rice soup
2 soup cans water
2 cups cooked shrimp, cut in small pieces
1 cup cooked cut green beans
  Dash cayenne pepper

Combine soups with water in saucepan. Mix in remaining ingredients and heat to serving temperature.

4 to 6 servings

Roquefort-Vegetable Salad

  Crisp salad greens
1 small onion, sliced
1 cup sliced raw cauliflower
1 can (16 ounces) cut green beans, chilled and drained
1 can (13 to 15 ounces) green asparagus spears, chilled and drained
  Roquefort-Mayonnaise Dressing (see recipe)
  Snipped parsley

1. Half-fill 6 individual salad bowls with the greens. Arrange vegetables on greens.

2. Accompany with a bowl of the dressing; garnish with parsley.

6 servings

Roquefort-Mayonnaise Dressing:

Blend 3 ounces cream cheese, softened, in a bowl with 3 ounces Roquefort cheese, crumbled. Stir in ½ cup half-and-half, ½ cup mayonnaise, ½ teaspoon Worcestershire sauce, ¼ teaspoon garlic powder, and ¼ teaspoon dry mustard. Beat until fluffy and chill.

About 1½ cups dressing

Chocolate Coconut Chews

48 (¾ pound) marshmallows
3 tablespoons butter or margarine
2 ounces (2 squares) unsweetened chocolate
4 cups (about 4 ounces) puffed rice or wheat, ready-to-eat oat cereal, or corn puffs
1 cup flaked coconut
1 teaspoon vanilla extract
½ teaspoon salt

1. Butter an 11×7×1½-inch pan.
2. Melt marshmallows, butter, and chocolate over simmering water, stirring occasionally.
3. Mix the cereal and coconut in a large buttered bowl; set aside.
4. Remove marshmallow mixture from heat. Mix in vanilla extract and salt.
5. Pour hot marshmallow mixture slowly over cereal mixture, stirring briskly to coat thoroughly. Turn mixture quickly into pan. Spread and press evenly to corners.
6. Chill in refrigerator about 1 hour, or until candy is firm. Cut into 2×1-inch bars.

About 3 dozen bars

DAY-SAILOR'S DELIGHT

Beef Brisket with Horseradish Sauce

Noodle-Cheese Casserole

Antipasto Salad

Fudge Oatmeal Squares   *Fruit*

Iced Tea   *Coffee*

Beef Brisket with Horseradish Sauce

1 fresh beef brisket (6 to 7 pounds)
4½ teaspoons seasoned salt
4 to 5 tablespoons all-purpose flour

½ cup chili sauce
½ cup ketchup
1 jar (5 ounces) prepared horseradish
1 cup boiling water

1. Sprinkle the beef with seasoned salt; coat evenly with flour. Set on a rack in a roasting pan. Roast at 450°F 30 minutes.
2. Combine the chili sauce, ketchup, and horseradish; mix well and spoon over meat.
3. Pour boiling water into bottom of pan; cover. Reduce oven temperature to 350°F and return meat to oven. Continue roasting about 3 hours, or until meat is tender.
4. If desired, thicken cooking liquid for gravy.

10 to 12 servings

Noodle-Cheese Casserole

1 package (8 ounces) fine noodles
6 ounces Swiss cheese, diced
¼ cup butter or margarine
½ cup chopped onion
1 cup dairy sour cream
1 teaspoon salt
½ teaspoon Worcestershire sauce

1. Cook and drain noodles.
2. Combine cheese, butter, and onion in a greased casserole. Turn drained noodles over mixture. Add sour cream, salt, and Worcestershire sauce; mix gently. Cover.
3. Cook in a 350°F oven 30 minutes. During the last 10 minutes of cooking remove cover.

4 to 6 servings

Antipasto Salad

- 1 quart assorted salad greens
- 1 package (10 ounces) frozen baby carrots in butter, cooked and drained
- 1 can (8¾ ounces) chickpeas or garbanzos, rinsed and drained
- 1 can (8¾ ounces) red kidney beans, rinsed and drained
- 1 jar (6 ounces) marinated artichoke hearts, drained and halved
- ½ cup sliced fresh mushrooms
- ½ cup drained pitted ripe olives
  Seasoned Walnuts (see recipe)
- 1 jar (4 ounces) pimento, cut in strips
- 8 slices cooked ham or ham luncheon loaf, cut in strips
  Dressing (see recipe)

1. Arrange greens on serving platter.
2. Atop greens, arrange carrots, chickpeas, kidney beans, artichokes, mushrooms, and olives in separate mounds around the edge. Center with Seasoned Walnuts.
3. Make divisions between mounds with pimento and ham strips. Serve with dressing.

6 to 8 servings

Seasoned Walnuts: In a skillet, brown 1 cup walnut halves in 1 tablespoon salad oil. Sprinkle with a dash each of garlic salt and thyme.

Dressing: Measure into a jar ¾ cup salad oil, ⅓ cup red wine vinegar, 1 tablespoon Parmesan cheese, 1 teaspoon seasoned salt, ½ teaspoon each basil, seasoned pepper, and dry mustard, and ¼ teaspoon garlic powder. Shake well.

About 1¼ cups dressing

Fudge Oatmeal Squares

- 2 ounces (2 squares) unsweetened chocolate
- ⅓ cup butter or margarine
- ¼ cup light corn syrup
- 2 teaspoons vanilla extract
- ¼ teaspoon salt
- ⅔ cup sugar
- 2 cups uncooked oats, quick or old-fashioned

- ½ cup coarsely chopped nuts

1. Melt chocolate and butter together in a saucepan over low heat.
2. Remove from heat. Add corn syrup, vanilla extract, salt, and sugar; mix well.
3. Stir in oats and nuts. Turn into a lightly greased 8-inch square pan.
4. Bake at 400°F 12 minutes. Remove the soft, bubbling mixture from oven. Set on a rack.
5. Cut into 2×1-inch bars while warm. Cool thoroughly in pan.

32 cookies

MARINA PARTY

Sailor's Borsch

Rémoulade with Scallops

Peekaboo Appetizers

Gourmet Gouda Spread

Cheddar-Sausage Rolls

Avocado Rye Rounds

Sailor's Borsch

- 1 can (46 ounces) tomato juice
- 1 tablespoon beef stock base
- 1 teaspoon salt
- 1 can or jar (16 ounces) sliced beets
- ⅓ cup coarsely chopped parsley
- 2 tablespoons red wine vinegar
- 1 carton (8 ounces) plain yogurt

1. Heat 1 cup tomato juice, beef stock base, and salt in a saucepan. Stir until beef stock base and salt are dissolved.
2. Combine 1 cup tomato juice with beets and liquid, parsley, and vinegar in an electric blender or a bowl; blend or beat until beets are finely chopped. Combine both mixtures with remaining tomato juice. Chill.
3. Top each serving with a dollop of yogurt.

About 2 quarts soup

Note: Borsch may be served hot. Yogurt may be stirred in just before serving, if desired.

Rémoulade with Scallops

1 cup dairy sour cream
1½ teaspoons prepared mustard
1½ teaspoons chopped capers
1½ teaspoons parsley flakes
1 teaspoon snipped chives
1 small clove garlic, crushed in a garlic press
Butter
1 package (12 ounces) frozen scallops, thawed and drained

1. Turn sour cream into a bowl. Gently blend in mustard, capers, parsley flakes, chives, and garlic. Cover and chill several hours or overnight.
2. Heat desired amount of butter in a skillet, add scallops, and sauté about 5 minutes, or until lightly browned. Serve on wooden picks with the sauce.

About 1 cup sauce

Peekaboo Appetizers

1 can (7¾ ounces) salmon, drained and flaked
⅓ cup dairy sour cream
⅓ cup finely chopped green pepper
2 tablespoons finely chopped onion
¼ teaspoon dill weed
¼ teaspoon salt
3 sticks pie crust mix
½ cup dairy sour cream
Toasted sesame seed

1. Combine salmon, ⅓ cup sour cream, green pepper, onion, dill weed, and salt in a bowl.
2. Meanwhile, prepare pastry according to package directions. Form into 3 balls; roll each into a

12×6-inch rectangle and cut into 18 squares. Place about 1 teaspoon filling in center of each square; bring corners together over filling and press pastry edges together. Place on a buttered baking sheet.
3. Bake at 450°F 12 minutes, or until lightly browned.
4. To serve, spoon about ½ teaspoon sour cream on each appetizer and top with sesame seed. Serve hot or cold.

54 appetizers

Gourmet Gouda Spread

1 round baby Gouda cheese (8 to 10 ounces) at room temperature
3 tablespoons blue cheese
2 tablespoons dry white wine
2 tablespoons butter
1 teaspoon prepared mustard
¼ teaspoon Worcestershire sauce

1. Cut top off Gouda cheese through red wax. Scoop out cheese, leaving a ¼-inch shell. Refrigerate shell.
2. Combine Gouda and blue cheeses in a small bowl; mix in wine, butter, mustard, and Worcestershire sauce. Fill shell with cheese mixture. Chill several hours or overnight.
3. Before serving, bring to room temperature. Accompany with crackers or party rye bread slices.

About 1 cup cheese spread

Cheddar-Sausage Rolls

1 cup (4 ounces) shredded Cheddar cheese, at room temperature
3 tablespoons dairy sour cream
6 slices summer sausage, about 4¼ inches in diameter

1. Combine cheese and sour cream in a small bowl.
2. Remove casings from sausage. Spread a scant 2 tablespoons cheese mixture on each slice of sausage. Place one slice of sausage on top of another, overlapping one half of the way. Roll sausage firmly and wrap. Repeat twice to form 3 rolls. Chill.
3. To serve, cut into ½-inch slices.

About 1½ dozen appetizers

Avocado Rye Rounds

½ cup cottage cheese
½ avocado, peeled and cut in pieces
1 tablespoon grated fresh onion
2 teaspoons fresh lemon juice
½ teaspoon Worcestershire sauce
3 drops Tabasco
¾ cup chopped cooked chicken
¼ cup chopped celery
Party rye bread slices, toasted and buttered
Pimento

1. Put cottage cheese and avocado into an electric blender or a bowl and blend or beat until fairly smooth. Blend in onion, lemon juice, Worcestershire sauce, and Tabasco. Stir in chicken and celery. Cover; chill several hours or overnight.
2. To serve, spread about 1 tablespoon avocado mixture on each rye toast slice. Garnish with pimento.

About 2 dozen appetizers

SOUPS

Creamy Frankfurter Soup

2 frankfurters, thinly sliced
2 tablespoons chopped onion
1 tablespoon butter or margarine
1 can (10¾ ounces) condensed tomato soup
1 soup can milk

1. Brown frankfurter slices and onion in butter.
2. Add soup and milk. Heat. Stir occasionally.

2 or 3 servings

Galley Soup Gourmet

2 cans (19 ounces each) chunky beef soup
¼ cup dairy sour cream
¼ cup Burgundy or other dry red wine

In saucepan, blend soup and sour cream. Add wine. Heat, stirring occasionally.

4 servings

Carrot-Pea Cream Soup

1 can (10½ ounces) condensed cream of chicken soup
1 can (11¼ ounces) condensed green pea soup
1½ cups milk
1 cup heavy cream
½ cup cooked sliced carrots
½ teaspoon grated onion
¼ teaspoon freshly ground black pepper
½ teaspoon ground thyme

1. Blend soups in a saucepan and gradually add milk and cream, stirring until well blended.
2. Add the remaining ingredients and heat thoroughly over medium heat, stirring occasionally.

4 to 6 servings

Vienna Bean-with-Bacon Bowl

1 can (11¼ ounces) condensed bean-with-bacon soup
1 can (10¾ ounces) condensed tomato soup
2 soup cans water
1 can (4 ounces) Vienna sausage

Blend soup in a saucepan; stir in water. Slice Vienna sausage; add to soup. Heat, stirring frequently.

4 servings

SANDWICHES

Sausage and Kraut Special

1 cup sauerkraut
½ teaspoon caraway seed
4 knockwurst (12 to 16 ounces), cooked
2 tablespoons mustard relish
4 hot dog buns, split and toasted

1. Combine sauerkraut and caraway seed in saucepan; heat.
2. Slit knockwurst and fill with mustard relish.
3. Place knockwurst in buns top with drained hot sauerkraut.

4 sandwiches

Chicken 'n' Chutney Sandwiches

6 slices raisin bread
1 package (3 ounces) cream cheese, softened
⅓ cup chopped chutney
3 servings sliced cooked chicken
   Butter or margarine, softened

1. Spread 3 slices bread with cream cheese, then chutney; top with chicken.

2. Butter remaining bread; cover sandwiches.

3 sandwiches

Yard-Long Sandwich

1 loaf French bread (1 pound)
½ cup butter or margarine
1 teaspoon prepared mustard
2 teaspoons prepared horseradish
2 tablespoons chopped parsley
8 slices bologna
8 slices pasteurized American or sharp
   Cheddar cheese
2 medium tomatoes, sliced
3 small dill pickles, sliced lengthwise

1. Cut loaf of bread into 1½-inch slices almost through to bottom. Using a sharp-pointed knife, remove alternate slices, leaving ¼ inch of the crust at bottom of loaf. Store alternate slices for other use. Place loaf on a baking sheet lined with aluminum foil.
2. Blend butter, mustard, horseradish, and parsley; spread over surfaces of each cut-out section of the loaf. Put into each cavity: one slice bologna, rolled, one slice of cheese, folded in half, one slice tomato, and one slice dill pickle.
3. Set in a 400°F oven about 10 minutes, or until cheese begins to melt and bread is thoroughly heated.
4. To serve, use very sharp knife to divide slices of bread in half, cutting through bottom crust to separate each sandwich. Use tongs to transfer to plates.

8 servings

CAMPSITE AND CAMPER COOKING

Economy—that's the bait that usually lures travelers to the camp trail, but it's enjoyment that keeps them there.

Camping means freedom from transportation schedules, hotel rates, and rules. And it puts you right into that beautiful scenery instead of into cramped, inner-city quarters. You're free to explore that big wide yonder, and live at your own pace.

PRACTICE MAKES PERFECT

In spite of all the pleasure it gives, it would be misleading to suggest that camping is all play. After all, you'll be working with infrequently-used equipment in unfamiliar settings. But the sheer novelty keeps it from being humdrum. And by following the example of seasoned campers, you can minimize the work and maximize the fun.

Before investing in outdoor cooking equipment, borrow or rent some. Have a trial run-through, cooking outdoors, to see what it's like. If you find it's for you, then make the investment, and have several more trial runs to get the feel of your equipment. It will make all the difference on the road.

Campsite cooking shouldn't be a one-man—or one-woman—job. Family participation is what's needed, and you'll probably find it's easier to get help at the campsite than back home.

DO YOUR HOMEWORK

Vacations are meant to be a break from work, so plan meals, figuring all possible shortcuts, before leaving. Homework time will save precious vacation hours.

You'll find help in the large paperback road guides and travel manuals in bookstores. They describe the campgrounds in all parts of the country and tell exactly what to expect in the way of camping facilities. Since these can range from poor to plush, it's best to be forewarned.

At the very minimum, you'll want water and sanitation facilities. Most families want shower accommodations. Luxurious, but not uncommon, are swimming pools and other recreational attractions. But if the countryside is interesting enough, you can make your own recreation.

EQUIPMENT FOR THE CAMP COOK

Most campgrounds have built-in grills, so you can plan to do some charcoal cooking without the bother of packing the brazier. The charcoal gives the good smoky flavor so prized by outdoor cooks, but the handy bottled gas stove you take along will give quicker results. And a fast meal is much in demand after a long day's drive.

The cooking equipment to pack depends upon what you'll be driving. Recreational vehicles often provide a homelike kitchen, needing only to be hooked into water and electricity outlets at the campground.

But if you're driving a car or station wagon, you'll need these basics:

FOR STORAGE

Cooler: metal or styrofoam. Buy block ice, or freeze your own in clean milk cartons. Use water when melted.

Pantry: purchased, or homemade from cardboard carton or plywood. Holds food and cooking equipment.

Thermos jug, kept up front for drinks while traveling.

Picnic basket, packed with table setting (see Picnicking chapter, p. 55).

FOR COOKING

Fold-up, two- or three-burner stove, fueled by unleaded gasoline, or propane or butane gas.

Griddle, and large skillet with lid.

Mixing bowls.

Cooking pans: aluminum nesting sets with two kettles on the outside, coffee pot, four pans and four cups inside, are handy.

Cooking tools: knives, stirring spoons, pancake turner, tongs, long forks for roasting marshmallows, skewers, hinged wire basket, colander, hot pads, long-handled popcorn popper.

FOR CLEANUP

Plastic pan or bucket, soap, abrasive pads, cloth, brush, cleansing powder, paper towels.

MEAL PLANNING

When vacationing, schedules get out of kilter, and you may be more active than usual. Meals that meet all your needs are a must. Meals, well planned and based on the four food groups, are in order (see chart, page 6).

But campsite meals should meet more than physical needs. Cooking and eating around the fire are a big part of what you'll remember from your trip.

An element of surprise is appreciated, as long as you stick with food your family likes.

Rely on old favorites, but give them a new look. Hamburger eaten in a taco shell becomes a new adventure. Crusty bread dipped into cheese fondue is an unexpected treat. Or chocolate candy rolls, melted over a campfire, makes a dessert fondue for dipping fruit chunks and leftover cake.

Here are menus for three days; try them some weekend before your big vacation. Make changes to suit preferences to they'll win your family's seal of approval. Just be sure to have a hearty breakfast each day, and fix lunches right after breakfast. Then you'll be free from cooking chores until dinner time.

MENUS FOR A THREE-DAY CAMPING TRIP

FIRST DAY

Breakfast
> At Home

Lunch
> Tuna Hoboes (page 87)
> Fresh Fruit
> Campsite Coffee (page 90)
> Milk

Dinner
> Skillet-Broiled Ham Slice with Pineapple (page 84)
> Sweet Potatoes   Green Beans
> Tossed Salad with French Dressing (page 88)
> Gold Cake with Broiled Coconut Topping (page 89)
> Coffee   Tea   Milk

SECOND DAY

Breakfast
> Orange Juice
> Bull's Eye Eggs (page 84)
> Toast   Jam
> Coffee   Milk

Lunch
> Assorted Sandwiches: Peanut Butter, Cheese, and Lunchmeat
> Fruit   Cookies
> Milk

Dinner
> Bedouin Beef with Rice Pilaf (page 82) on Pita Bread or Wheat Tortillas (page 87)
> Vegetable Accompaniments
> Yogurt or Sour Cream Topping
> Some-Mores (page 89)
> Tea   Milk

THIRD DAY

Breakfast
> Melon Strips
> French Toast (page 86)   Syrup
> Coffee   Milk

Lunch
> Cheese and Meat Roll-Ups on Buns (page 88)
> Cucumber and Carrot Strips
> Candy Bars   Milk

Dinner
> Poached Fish with Camper's Hollandaise (page 84)
> Instant Mashed Potatoes
> Asparagus

Savory Rice Pilaf; Spit-Roasted Cornish Hens;
Fresh Sweet Cherry Appetizer Tray

Tossed Salad with French Dressing (page 88)
Leftover Cake and Fruit Dunked in Chocolate Candy Fondue (page 90)
Coffee   Milk

GETTING READY FOR THE TRIP

If you're like most campers, you "think vacation" all year. You make note of recipes that sound right for outdoors, and you squirrel away such things as empty coffee cans and plastic cartons. At packing time, you can transfer staples into them for lightweight, waterproof storage. Just be sure to label containers, and clip mixing instructions such as those on biscuit mix and milk solids to pack right in with the food.

Empty plastic honey bottles, the kind with the squirt top, are great to carry vegetable oil. At cooking time, a quick squeeze will grease the skillet or baking pan. Plastic bags serve many uses, too.

Matches should have a special place where you can find them quickly. You can waterproof matches by dipping them in paraffin or coating with nail polish.

Pack a few bright bandanas. They do double and triple duty as table mats, napkins, aprons, and towels—and they look nice, too!

HOW LONG WILL THE FOOD KEEP?

Vacation time is no time to take chances on food that is past its peak. It's a good idea to take only what fresh meat you can eat the first day. Unless you're leaving civilization entirely behind, you can find supermarkets or campground trading posts nearly everywhere.

If you wish, you can take frozen meat or frozen cooked dishes, in your cooler. They will help to keep the other food cold, and by the second day will be ready to cook and eat.

Lunchmeat, ham, and franks should be used within two to three days. Bacon will keep up to a week in the cooler.

Hard, dry sausages such as salami and peperoni keep without refrigeration before cutting. Once cut, store them in the cooler.

Time isn't the hazard for some staples, such as salt and sugar. Moisture is the villain, so keep dry foods in watertight containers.

CAMPSITE COOKING

Once you're familiar with controlling the small gas stove, cooking proceeds much as it does at home.

But where you are can make a big difference. If you're heading for the hills, remember that altitude affects cooking times. It will probably seem that the pot will never boil, watched or not. Adjust your menus accordingly, and allow plenty of time for anything that requires boiling water. Save baking for back home.

CLEANUP

Neatness counts everywhere, but especially at the campsite. At home you know approximately where everything is, but at camp things are in a new framework. Once you've arranged them into the camp pantry, try to keep them there. It will make getting the next meal much easier.

A trip across our country's campgrounds will convince you that most campers are lovers of the land who treat it with concern. Most have cleaned the area behind them, respecting the campers who will follow.

Good camp-keeping means burning all combustible garbage and disposing of the rest at designated garbage drop-offs. Liquids should be thrown out in an arc in some untrafficked area, or poured into a ditch and covered with dirt or sand.

Smoky the Bear has probably already indoctrinated you, but it *bears* repeating: Don't go off and leave a campfire burning. Don't let a fire burn while you sleep. Extinguish it by drowning, stir the ashes, and drown again. Embers should be cool before you leave the site.

TOP: Avocado Rye Rounds; Peekaboo Appetizers; Rémoulade with Scallops; Cheddar-Sausage Rolls; Gourmet Gouda Spread; Sailor's Borsch
BOTTOM: Corn on the Grill; Barbecued Spareribs à la Marinade

MAIN DISHES
FREEZE AT HOME—
REHEAT AT CAMPSITE

Some dishes have special appeal for campers, yet take too long to prepare at campsite. Cook these at home, freeze, and take one along in your cooler chest. It will help keep the other foods cold, and give you a great meal the second day out.

Chicken à la King

½ pound mushrooms
⅓ cup butter, margarine, or chicken fat
¼ cup chopped green pepper
¼ cup all-purpose flour
1 teaspoon salt
Few grains pepper
1½ cups half-and-half
2 chicken bouillon cubes
1½ cups boiling water
3 cups chopped cooked chicken
¼ cup canned pimento, cut in strips

1. Clean and slice mushrooms. Heat butter in a heavy skillet with cover; add mushrooms and green pepper. Cook over low heat about 5 minutes. With slotted spoon, lift out vegetables, allowing fat to drain back into skillet; set vegetables aside.
2. Stir flour, salt, and pepper into fat in skillet. Cook until mixture bubbles. Remove from heat. Stir in half-and-half.
3. Dissolve bouillon cubes in boiling water. Blend into mixture in skillet. Bring to boiling; cook and stir 1 to 2 minutes.
4. Stir chopped chicken into skillet mixture along with reserved vegetables and pimento.

5. Cool and pack in container. Store in the freezer.
6. At campsite, cook over low heat, stirring occasionally, until heated through. Serve on hot rice or canned chow mein noodles.

8 servings

Ground Meat in Barbecue Sauce

1 cup ketchup
½ cup water
2 tablespoons sugar
2 tablespoons prepared mustard
2 tablespoons vinegar
2 teaspoons Worcestershire sauce
2 tablespoons butter or margarine
1 cup chopped onion
2 pounds ground beef
2 teaspoons salt
½ teaspoon pepper

1. For barbecue sauce, combine ketchup, water, sugar, mustard, vinegar, and Worcestershire sauce in a 1-pint screw-top jar. Cover and shake until blended.
2. For meat mixture, heat butter in a skillet. Add onion and cook until tender. Add ground beef, breaking apart with spoon. Mix in seasonings. When meat is browned, blend in sauce. Cook over low heat about 15 minutes.
3. Cool and pack into container. Store in the freezer.
4. At campsite, cook over low heat, stirring occasionally. Serve on buttered buns.

4 to 6 servings

Bedouin Beef with Rice Pilaf

1½ pounds beef for stew, cut in ½-inch cubes
1½ tablespoons salad or cooking oil
1 small onion, chopped
1 clove garlic, minced
1 can (13¾ ounces) chicken broth
1 tablespoon lemon juice
⅛ teaspoon ground allspice
1 small cinnamon stick
1 cup cooked rice
Pita (mideast) bread, split, or Wheat Tortillas (page 87)
Vegetable Accompaniments (below)
Yogurt or dairy sour cream

1. In a Dutch oven, brown meat in oil. Add onion and garlic; cook until tender.

2. Stir in broth, lemon juice, allspice, and cinnamon stick. Cover and simmer about 45 minutes, or until meat is tender.

3. Add rice; cover and heat thoroughly. Remove from heat; cool.

4. When cooled to room temperature, pack into freezer container and freeze.

5. At campsite, reheat. Let campers assemble their own, spooning the hot beef-rice mixture into split pita (mideast) bread or on wheat tortillas. Sprinkle Vegetable Accompaniments over the meat mixture and top with a dollop of yogurt or sour cream.

6 to 8 servings

Vegetable Accompaniments: Cut an avocado and a tomato into wedges and a green pepper into strips. Chop green onions and lettuce. Arrange vegetables in separate mounds on paper plates.

Barbecued Meat Loaf

  1 egg, fork beaten
1½ to 2 teaspoons salt
  1 teaspoon Worcestershire sauce
  1 can (8 ounces) tomato sauce
¾ cup hickory-flavor ketchup
¾ cup fine dry bread crumbs
  1 cup finely chopped onion
1½ pounds lean ground beef
½ pound bulk pork sausage

1. Combine egg, salt, and Worcestershire sauce. Add tomato sauce and ½ cup of the ketchup, blending thoroughly. Mix in bread crumbs and onion.

2. With a fork, lightly mix in a blend of the meats. Form into loaf shape in a shallow baking pan or lightly pack into a loaf pan.

3. Bake at 350°F 1 hour. Drain off fat and pour remaining ¼ cup ketchup over loaf. Continue baking 30 minutes.

4. Cool meat loaf slightly, cut into thick slices, wrap in foil, and freeze until time to pack.

5. At campsite, brush ketchup on meat loaf slices and heat on grill.

6 servings

Note: Meat mixture may be shaped into patties, wrapped individually in foil, and frozen until ready to pack. At campsite, unwrap patties and place in hinged basket broiler or on prepared grill. Grill about 5 inches from coals, 4 minutes on each side, or until done as desired. Baste with ketchup during grilling.

Chop Suey

  3 tablespoons fat
1¼ pounds boneless pork, cut in strips
  1 pound boneless beef, cut in strips
¾ pound boneless veal, cut in strips
1½ cups coarsely chopped onion
  3 cups diagonally sliced celery
  1 can (8 ounces) mushrooms, drained; reserve liquid
  1 can (16 ounces) bean sprouts, drained; reserve liquid
  1 can (5 ounces) water chestnuts, drained and thinly sliced
¼ cup cornstarch
  1 teaspoon salt
  1 teaspoon monosodium glutamate
½ cup soy sauce
¼ cup bead molasses

1. Heat fat in a heavy skillet with cover; add meat and brown over medium heat, turning pieces occasionally. Cover and cook over low heat 1 hour.

2. Stir in onion, celery, mushrooms, bean sprouts, and water chestnuts. Add ½ cup each of the reserved mushroom and bean sprout liquids; cook, covered, over low heat 20 minutes longer.

3. Combine cornstarch, salt, and monosodium glutamate in a bowl. Mix in ½ cup of the reserved bean sprout liquid, soy sauce, and molasses. Stir into meat mixture and bring to boiling; cook 10 to 15 minutes longer, occasionally turning mixture with a fork.

4. Cool and pack into containers. Store in freezer.

5. At campsite, cook over low heat, turning occasionally, until heated through. Serve on rice or bread slices.

8 to 10 servings

MAIN DISHES
PREPARE AT CAMPSITE

Campfire Fondue

- **1 can (10¾ ounces) condensed Cheddar cheese soup**
- **1 package (6 ounces) Swiss cheese, shredded**
- **½ teaspoon prepared mustard**
  Few grains cayenne pepper

1. In a small saucepan, heat cheese soup and shredded Swiss cheese until cheese is melted. Add seasonings. Stir frequently to prevent sticking.
2. To eat the fondue, dip cubes of French bread or pieces of rusks into the hot cheese mixture.

4 servings

Poached Fish with Camper's Hollandaise

- **1½ pounds fish fillets, such as perch or bass**
  Boiling water
- **2 tablespoons minced onion**
- **2 teaspoons parsley flakes**
- **1 teaspoon salt**
- **½ teaspoon pepper**

1. Tie fish loosely in cheesecloth to prevent breaking; place in a 10-inch skillet with a tight-fitting cover.
2. Add boiling water to cover and seasonings.
3. Cover skillet and simmer about 10 minutes, or until fish is fork tender. Serve with Camper's Hollandaise.

4 servings

Camper's Hollandaise
- **8 tablespoons (1 stick) butter**
- **2 egg yolks (save whites for scrambled eggs)**
- **1 teaspoon Dijon-style mustard**
- **1 tablespoon lemon juice**

1. Melt 1 tablespoon butter in a small frying pan over low heat; remove from heat.

2. Stir egg yolks and mustard smoothly into butter.
3. On prongs of fork, spear remaining 7 tablespoons firm butter and replace pan over low heat. Stir rapidly as it melts, blending throughout egg mixture until sauce thickens slightly.
4. Remove pan from heat and stir in lemon juice.

⅔ cup sauce

Skillet-Broiled Ham Slice with Pineapple

- **2 ham slices, ½ inch thick**
- **1 can (13¼ ounces) crushed pineapple (undrained)**

1. Place ham slices in a heavy skillet. Cook over low heat, turning occasionally, until meat is tender (about 15 minutes).
2. Top with crushed pineapple; cover and cook 5 minutes longer, or until pineapple is hot.

4 to 6 servings

Bull's Eye Eggs

- **Butter or margarine**
- **1 slice bread**
- **1 egg**

1. Butter bread on both sides. Cut a round from center of bread.
2. Heat some butter in a skillet just hot enough to

sizzle a drop of water. Place bread (frame and round) in skillet.

3. Break egg into hole in bread. Cook over low heat until egg is set and bread is browned. Turn; brown other side.

4. Serve toast round with egg in toast frame. Repeat for as many servings as desired.

1 serving

Skillet Luncheon Meat Surprise

1 can (8 ounces) tomato sauce
1 can (16 ounces) sliced peaches, drained; reserve ¼ cup syrup
2 tablespoons lemon juice
1 to 2 tablespoons prepared horseradish
½ teaspoon Worcestershire sauce
¼ cup packed brown sugar
1 teaspoon dry mustard
½ teaspoon salt
1 can (12 ounces) luncheon meat, cut in ¼-inch slices
¼ cup thin sweet pickle slices

1. In a large skillet, combine tomato sauce, peach syrup, lemon juice, horseradish, Worcestershire sauce, brown sugar, dry mustard, and salt. Cover and simmer 5 minutes.

2. Add meat, peaches, and pickles to mixture in skillet; spoon sauce over all.

3. Cover and simmer until thoroughly heated.

About 4 servings

Can-Can Quickie

1 can (17 ounces) whole kernel corn
1 can (12 ounces) luncheon meat
¼ cup bottled barbecue sauce

1. Empty corn into a skillet. Cut meat into 8 slices and arrange on corn.

2. Pour barbecue sauce over meat.

3. Cover skillet and cook on low heat about 15 to 20 minutes, or until meat is heated through.

4 servings

Note: Use lima beans or peas instead of corn. Substitute 1 can (10½ ounces) condensed cream of celery, chicken, or mushroom soup or 1 can (10¾ ounces) tomato soup for barbecue sauce. Heat.

Meat, Green Bean, and Blue Cheese Combo

Substitute green beans for corn in recipe for Can-Can Quickie. Spread pasteurized blue cheese spread (5-ounce jar) on sliced meat before arranging meat over beans. Heat.

Frankly Outdoor Stew

1 pound frankfurters, cut in ½-inch chunks
2 tablespoons minced onion
½ clove garlic, minced (optional)
¾ cup coarsely chopped pitted ripe olives
1 can (6 ounces) tomato juice
1 teaspoon Worcestershire sauce
½ teaspoon celery salt
1 can (16 ounces) kidney beans, drained and rinsed
1 can (16 ounces) whole kernel corn
1 cup shredded Cheddar cheese

1. Combine franks, onion, garlic, olives, tomato juice, seasonings, and vegetables in a large saucepan. Cook over medium heat until thoroughly heated.

2. Remove from heat; add cheese and stir until melted.

3. Serve on buttered slices of French bread or rusks.

6 servings

Tunaroni

1 can (6½ or 7 ounces) tuna, drained and
  flaked
1 can (15 ounces) macaroni and cheese
½ cup (2 ounces) cubed mild Cheddar cheese
1 teaspoon instant minced onion
¼ teaspoon salt
1 tablespoon lemon juice (optional)

Combine all ingredients in a saucepan. Set over
medium heat, stirring occasionally, just until
thoroughly heated. Serve immediately.

4 servings

Scrambled
Eggs and Peppers
in Bologna Cups

1 chub bologna
2 tablespoons cooking oil or margarine
1 small green pepper, diced
2 packages (2.2 ounce size each) freeze-dried
  scrambled egg mix
1 cup water

1. Cut 4 slices of bologna about ¼ inch thick.
2. In skillet, fry bologna slices in oil, turning
once, until slices "cup." Set aside in a warm place.
3. Sauté green pepper in bologna drippings.
4. Add water to both packages of scrambled egg
mix; blend with fork. Pour into skillet containing
green pepper and scramble as desired.
5. Spoon egg mixture into bologna cups and
serve.

4 servings

BREADS

French Toast

2 eggs, slightly beaten
⅔ cup milk
1 tablespoon sugar
½ teaspoon salt
3 to 4 tablespoons butter or margarine
8 slices bread

1. Combine eggs with milk, sugar, and salt in a
pie pan.
2. Heat some of the butter in a skillet.
3. Dip bread slices one at a time into egg mixture,
coating each side well. Transfer to heated skillet.
Brown slices over medium heat, turning once.
Add butter as needed to keep from sticking.
4. Serve with butter and syrup, honey, jam, or
confectioners' sugar.

8 slices French toast

Bread on a Stick

2 cups all-purpose biscuit mix
½ cup water

1. Combine biscuit mix and water. Mix with a
fork to form a soft dough.
2. Strip bark from one end of a green stick, one
for each camper.
3. Pinch off a small portion of dough, mold it into
a long patty, and wrap it around the stick in a
spiral twist. Be sure that the dough covers the end
of the stick so there will be a closed end. Press
cracks together.
4. Place on grill over low heat and bake about 20
minutes, turning often.
5. When done, slip off stick, and fill the hole with
butter and jelly. For a hot sandwich, fill with diced
cheese or peanut butter.

12 servings

Clothespin
Coffeecake

1 package (14½ ounces) nut bread mix (such
  as blueberry, cranberry, banana)

1. Soak six spring-type clothespins in water.

2. Generously grease two 9-inch aluminum foil pans.

3. Prepare bread mix according to package directions. Turn batter into one pan. Invert other pan over first pan. Secure pans with clothespins.

4. Place on grill 3 to 4 inches from hot coals. Cook 30 minutes, turning over once and rotating pan occasionally for even baking.

5. Remove cover and insert wooden pick. If it comes out clean, cake is done. If not, replace cover and cook until done.

6. Remove cover. Slice and serve from pan.

About 6 servings

Wheat Tortillas

3 cups all-purpose biscuit mix
¾ cup warm water

1. Combine mix and water; form into a ball. Knead about 60 times, or until ball is smooth. Cover; let rest 5 minutes.

2. Divide ball into 12 portions. Shape into balls and roll out, or form into patties by rotating in the heel of the hand until surface is smooth. Let rest 5 minutes.

3. Heat a griddle just hot enough to sizzle a drop of water.

4. Prepare patties one at a time, rolling on unfloured surface until each is about 6 inches in diameter, and as thin as pastry.

5. Drop tortillas, one at a time, on griddle. Turn each immediately; this prevents sticking. As tortillas turn brown at edges, turn them over. When brown on both sides, tortillas are done.

6. To serve, butter tortillas and use as bread with a meal, or top with jelly or cheese for snack. Or serve topped with meat in sauce, such as stew.

12 tortillas

Note: To improvise a rolling pin, use an unopened can with paper label removed. A large jar or tumbler will also work.

SANDWICHES

Dried Beef-Cream Cheese Sandwiches

1 package (3 ounces) cream cheese (room temperature)
⅓ cup (about 1 ounce) chopped dried beef
1 tablespoon prepared horseradish (optional)
Few drops Worcestershire sauce
8 slices bread

1. Mash cream cheese with a fork. Stir in chopped dried beef and combine thoroughly. Add horseradish, if desired, and Worcestershire sauce.

2. Spread on 4 bread slices. Top with remaining bread.

4 sandwiches

Tuna Hoboes

1 loaf Italian bread (about 15 inches long), cut in half lengthwise
Butter or margarine
Lettuce leaves
Tuna Salad (see recipe)
Sliced tomato
Sliced sweet onion
½ pound assorted sliced luncheon meat
¼ pound sliced American cheese
Cherry tomatoes, pimento-stuffed olives (optional)

1. On cut surface of each bread half, spread butter. Cover with lettuce. Top with Tuna Salad, tomato, onion, meat, and cheese.

2. If desired, spear cherry tomatoes and olives with wooden picks and use to garnish sandwiches.

6 to 8 servings

Tuna Salad: Mix 2 cans (6½ or 7 ounces each) tuna, drained and flaked, ¼ cup sweet pickle relish, and 6 tablespoons mayonnaise.

The Virginian Sandwich

8 to 12 slices pumpernickel, rye, or whole wheat bread
Soft butter
1 jar (5 ounces) pasteurized process cheese spread with pineapple
¼ cup chopped peanuts
8 to 12 slices cooked ham (about 8 ounces)
Bibb or iceberg lettuce

1. Spread bread slices with soft butter.
2. Combine cheese spread and peanuts in a bowl; mix thoroughly. Spread on half the bread slices.
3. Top with ham, lettuce, and remaining bread slices.

4 to 6 sandwiches

Meat 'n' Cheese Sandwiches

1 package (3 ounces) cream cheese (room temperature)
1 teaspoon prepared mustard
½ teaspoon dried chives
8 slices bread
Thin slices salami, dried beef, or ham

1. Mash cream cheese with a fork. Stir in mustard and chives; combine thoroughly.
2. Spread cheese mixture on 4 bread slices. Top with meat slices and remaining bread.

4 sandwiches

Cheese and Meat Roll-Ups on Buns

½ pound Cheddar or Swiss cheese
½ pound sliced salami, summer sausage, or other luncheon meat
8 frankfurter buns
Butter
Ketchup, mayonnaise, prepared mustard
Lettuce leaves (optional)

1. Cut cheese lengthwise into 8 strips. Wrap meat slices around cheese strips.

2. Open buns and spread with butter and choice of condiments.
3. Put cheese-meat roll-ups inside buns. Add lettuce, if desired, and serve.

8 sandwiches

Note: Dieters may prefer to eat the cheese-meat roll-ups as finger food, omitting buns.

SALADS

Stuffed Tomato Salad

3 large tomatoes
1 pound cottage cheese
½ teaspoon paprika
Few grains pepper
½ cup mayonnaise
Lettuce cups

1. Cut tomatoes in half and scoop pulp into mixing bowl.
2. Season cottage cheese with paprika and pepper.
3. Fill tomato shells with seasoned cottage cheese; place in lettuce cups.
4. Mix tomato pulp with mayonnaise and serve as dressing for salad.

6 servings

Seasoning Mix for French Dressing

⅓ cup sugar
¼ cup salt
3 tablespoons instant minced onion
4 teaspoons paprika
1 teaspoon dry mustard

Combine ingredients and store in a small tightly covered container.

French Dressing

Combine 1 cup salad oil, ¼ cup vinegar, and 1 tablespoon Seasoning Mix for French Dressing in a 1-pint jar. Shake until blended. Serve on tossed greens.

Fruit French Dressing

Combine ½ cup salad oil, ¼ cup honey, ¼ cup orange juice, 2 tablespoons lemon juice, and 1 tablespoon Seasoning Mix for French Dressing. Shake well and pour over fruit salad.

Blue Cheese Dressing

Make French Dressing and add ¼ cup crumbled blue cheese. Serve on vegetable salad.

DESSERTS

Gold Cake with Broiled Topping

    2 cups sifted cake flour
1¼ cups sugar
2½ teaspoons baking powder
    ½ teaspoon salt
    1 cup milk
    ½ cup vegetable shortening
    1 teaspoon lemon extract
    ½ teaspoon vanilla extract
    4 egg yolks, unbeaten
      Coconut Topping (see recipe)

1. Grease bottom of a 13×9×2-inch baking pan.

2. Sift together into a large bowl the flour, sugar, baking powder, and salt.
3. Add ⅔ cup of the milk to the dry ingredients along with the shortening and lemon and vanilla extracts. Stir only to moisten.
4. Beat 200 strokes by hand or 2 minutes on electric mixer at medium speed. Scrape sides of bowl several times during beating.
5. Add remaining milk and egg yolks. Beat 200 strokes by hand or 2 minutes on electric mixer, scraping sides of bowl several times. Pour batter into pan.
6. Bake at 350°F 30 to 35 minutes, or until cake springs back and leaves no indentation when touched lightly at center. Set on rack about 10 minutes.
7. Spread Coconut Topping on warm cake and place under broiler. Heat until topping is lightly browned and bubbly, about 2 minutes.

One 13×9-inch cake

Coconut Topping: Combine ½ cup butter or margarine, melted, 1 cup firmly packed brown sugar, 1⅓ cups (about) flaked coconut, ⅓ cup half-and-half, and ½ teaspoon vanilla extract. Let stand 5 minutes.

Angel Halos

  6 doughnuts
  6 marshmallows

1. String doughnuts sideways onto skewers and put a marshmallow inside each doughnut hole.
2. Roast over grill, taking care that the doughnuts do not get too close to the heat. When marshmallows are soft and golden, the halos are ready to serve.

6 servings

Some-Mores

12 marshmallows
24 square graham crackers
 4 milk chocolate bars (1½ ounces each), broken in thirds

1. Toast marshmallows to golden brown.
2. Assemble Some-Mores, sandwich fashion, with a toasted marshmallow and chocolate piece between graham crackers. Gently press together.

12 servings

Chocolate Candy Fondue

2 cups cut-up chewy chocolate candy sticks
¼ cup water
   Dippers for fondue such as cubed pound cake, marshmallows, fruit chunks

1. Combine candy pieces and water in a small heavy saucepan. Melt over low heat, stirring occasionally. If mixture seems too thick, add a little more water.
2. Arrange cake cubes, marshmallows, and fruit chunks on a serving plate.
3. Use sharpened twigs or long-handled forks for dipping.

About 1 cup fondue

BEVERAGE

Campsite Coffee

4½ cups cold water
10 tablespoons ground coffee
¼ cup cold water
⅛ teaspoon salt

1. Bring 4½ cups water to a rolling boil. Remove from heat.
2. Add coffee; simmer slowly 8 minutes.
3. Add cold water and salt. Serve as soon as coffee is clear.

4 servings

BACKPACK MEALS

"Less is more" are golden words of advice for the backpacker. Every ounce counts when you're carrying everything from food to bedding and clothing on your back. The lighter and more carefully organized the load, the better.

Because of the physical exertion, backpackers have great need for nutritious meals. But just because of that activity, they may have the least energy and inclination to do an ambitious cooking job. So, if you're contemplating a pack trip, do some careful planning beforehand.

PLANNING FOR THE CAMP TRIP

If you're new to backpacking, visit a sporting goods store and see what's available. Ask other backpackers for advice. Where you're going and the length of your trip will determine what you'll need. Modern, lightweight metals and fabrics make it possible to pack an incredible amount of gear, but you'll want to tailor your purchases to your individual plans.

Take a look at the freeze-dried and dehydrated foods especially packaged for campers. You'll probably find an assortment as varied as that offered by a gourmet restaurant, so making meals-on-the-go interesting is no problem. And many of those items are packed in containers that double as cookers, helping to reduce your load. But you pay for that convenience. Before making final decisions, check your supermarket to see what dried foods are available in regular brands. You might have to switch those everyday foods into smaller, lightweight containers, and measure smaller cooking quantities into plastic bags. But the savings could make the effort worthwhile.

After you see what's available, make meal plans according to that old reliable, the basic four food groups (see page 6).

PLANNING BACKPACK MENUS

Certain foods fit into those four groups particularly well for the pack trip. Here are some suggestions:

1. *Meat group.* Hard dry sausages such as salami and peperoni require no refrigeration before they are cut. Beef jerky is a dried meat long used on the trail. Cheese and small cans of meat and fish, such as tuna, are complete protein sources.

2. *Milk.* Nonfat dry milk is the backpacker's standby.

3. *Fruits and vegetables.* Dried fruits and nuts are excellent. If you know your plants, you can add fresh crunch to meals with such things as dandelion greens.

4. *Bread sticks, toast rusks, and crackers all keep well.* Instant cooked cereals are handy.

It helps to test dehydrated foods, or anything different from your regular diet, at home. If the food isn't to your taste, you may want to add small packets of seasonings to your food bag.

WATER: YOUR LIFE DEPENDS ON IT

The water to drink on the trail can be carried in a canteen, but you'll need a water source at mealtime for cooking and cleanup. If you're not sure about the safety of your water, boil it for ten minutes or treat it with a purifier, such as halazone tablets, used as the package directs. Purified water tastes best combined with some flavoring mix such as that used to make chocolate milk, citrus juice, or iced tea.

GIVE BACKPACKING A ROAD TEST

Have a trial run before leaving home. Pack all

your gear, and hike around the block with a full load to see how it sits. Chances are, you'll come back and toss out some items to lighten the load. Be ready to adjust your menu in order to make hiking more enjoyable.

BACKPACKER'S BREAKFAST

Sliced Strawberries and Oranges

Backpacker's Eggs Olé

Milk (reconstituted dry)   *Coffee*

Sliced Strawberries and Oranges

**1 envelope (1 ounce) freeze-dried
    strawberries**
3 oranges

1. Following package directions, cut open and form a bowl of the plastic bag holding strawberries.
2. Peel, section, and cut oranges over strawberries, allowing juice to drip onto the berries. (This juice will reconstitute strawberries.) Mix fruit. Let stand for 10 minutes, stirring occasionally.

4 servings

Backpacker's Eggs Olé

**2 containers (2 or 2.2 ounces each)
    freeze-dried scrambled egg mix**
1 cup cold water
1 small chub salami
4 slices white bread
1 can (4 ounces) taco sauce

1. To scrambled egg mix, add cold water; blend with a fork to mix.
2. Cut salami chub into 8 slices; fry on griddle over medium-hot fire. Wrap and keep warm at edge of fire.
3. Pour grease into an empty can; reserve.

4. Dip bread into egg mixture. Fry on both sides on griddle until golden brown, as for French toast. Wrap in aluminum foil and keep warm at edge of fire.
5. Add a little grease to griddle. Cook and scramble remaining egg mixture.
6. Heat opened can of taco sauce at edge of fire.
7. To serve, place a slice of French toast on each plate. Top with 2 salami slices, scrambled eggs, and a little taco sauce.

4 servings

KNAPSACK LUNCH

Sliced Rye Bread

Swiss Cheese   *Dried Apricots*

Beef Jerky

Wheat-Flake Bars

Reconstituted Dried Fruit Drink

Beef Jerky

1 pound very lean top round steak
4 teaspoons salt
1 teaspoon pepper
1 teaspoon chili powder
1 teaspoon garlic powder
1 teaspoon onion powder
¼ teaspoon cayenne pepper
3 dashes liquid smoke
½ cup water

1. Trim the meat, removing any fat or connective tissue, and place in the freezer to freeze partially (about 1 hour).
2. Meanwhile, mix the salt, pepper, chili powder, garlic powder, onion powder, cayenne, and liquid smoke in a bowl. Add water and stir to blend.
3. When the meat has firmed enough to slice easily, cut across the grain in slanting slices about ⅛ inch thick. Put the strips into the marinade, stir, cover, and chill several hours or overnight, stirring occasionally.
4. Remove strips from marinade, drain, and spread on wire racks placed on baking sheets. Place in a 200°F oven with door slightly ajar. Dry

until a piece cracks when bent but does not break in two (5½ to 6 hours).

5. Cool on racks, then store in a covered container at room temperature or in the refrigerator.

About 8 ounces jerky

Wheat-Flake Bars

- 2 cups whole wheat cereal flakes
- 2 cups sifted enriched all-purpose flour
- 1 teaspoon baking powder
- ¾ cup firmly packed brown sugar
- ¾ cup plus 2 tablespoons butter or margarine, chilled
- ½ cup orange marmalade
  Glossy Orange Frosting (see recipe)
  Semisweet chocolate pieces

1. Mix cereal, flour, baking powder, and brown sugar in a bowl. Cut in butter until crumbly.
2. Press about two-thirds of the mixture in an even layer on the bottom of a 13×9×2-inch pan. Spread with marmalade; sprinkle remaining cereal mixture over marmalade.
3. Bake at 350°F about 30 minutes. Remove to a wire rack. Cool completely.
4. Frost with Glossy Orange Frosting. Cut into 3×1-inch bars. Decorate each bar with three semisweet chocolate pieces (points up).

3 dozen cookies

Glossy Orange Frosting: Beat one egg white slightly; beat in 1½ cups confectioners' sugar. Add 1 tablespoon melted butter or margarine, ⅛ teaspoon salt, 1 teaspoon vanilla extract, and ¼ teaspoon orange extract; beat until smooth. Blend in, one drop at a time, orange food coloring (a mixture of about 2 drops of red and 6 drops of yellow) until frosting is tinted a light orange.

About 1 cup frosting

SUNDOWN SUPPER

Trailblazer's Tuna-Mac Dinner

Wild Greens Salad

Rye Bread

Peanut Butter Bars   *Dates*

Hot Coffee or Hot Cocoa

Trailblazer's Tuna-Mac Dinner

- 1 package (7½ ounces) macaroni and cheese dinner
- 2 tablespoons instant nonfat dry milk
- ¼ cup plus 2 tablespoons water
- 1 can (6½ or 7 ounces) tuna in oil

1. Prepare macaroni and cheese dinner according to package directions, using dry milk liquefied in water for milk.
2. Mix in tuna, including oil from can to substitute for butter in package directions.
3. Heat a few minutes until tuna is hot and serve.

4 servings

Peanut Butter Bars

- 1¼ cups sifted all-purpose flour
- 2 teaspoons baking powder
- ¼ teaspoon salt
- ½ cup butter or margarine
- ½ cup peanut butter
- 1½ teaspoons vanilla extract
- ½ cup firmly packed brown sugar
- ½ cup sugar
- 1 egg

1. Sift flour, baking powder, and salt together; set aside.
2. Cream butter, peanut butter, and vanilla extract until thoroughly blended.
3. Add sugars gradually, creaming until fluffy after each addition.
4. Add egg and beat thoroughly.
5. Thoroughly blend in dry ingredients. Turn into 15×10×1-inch pan and spread evenly.
6. Bake at 375°F about 20 minutes. Cut into 3×1½-inch bars while warm. Remove to racks to cool.

2½ dozen bars

INDEX